GOD'S TOP 10

Blowing the Lid Off
the Commandments

GOD'S TOP 10

Blowing the Lid Off the Commandments

ANNE ROBERTSON

www.annerobertson.com

MOREHOUSE PUBLISHING

HARRISBURG / PENNSYLVANIA

Morehouse Publishing, P.O. Box 1321, Harrisburg, PA 17105
Morehouse Publishing, 445 Fifth Avenue, New York, NY 10016
Morehouse Publishing is an imprint of Church Publishing Incorporated.

Cover design by David Fiore and Weiqin Bao
Interior design by Beth Oberholtzer

Library of Congress Cataloging-in-Publication Data

Robertson, Anne, 1959-
God's top 10 : blowing the lid off the commandments / Anne Robertson.
    p.   cm.
Includes bibliographical references.
ISBN-13: 978-0-8192-2215-2 (pbk.)
1. Ten commandments—Criticism, interpretation, etc. I. Title.
BS1285.52.R63   2006
241.5'2—dc22

                                        2006022317

Printed in the United States of America

06 07 08 09   10 9 8 7 6 5 4 3 2 1

To any voter who has ever cited
"moral values" as the reason
for their political choice.

Contents

Acknowledgments viii

Introduction ix

1. No Other Gods 1

2. No Graven Images 15

3. Taking God's Name in Vain 29

4. Remember the Sabbath 39

5. Honor Thy Father and Mother 53

6. Life and Death 67

7. Be Faithful 89

8. Whose Is It, Anyway? 113

9. False Witness 133

10. Thou Shalt Not Covet 153

11. What Does the Lord Require? 165

Notes 171

Further Reading 177

Acknowledgments

Thank you to all who took time to read and comment on portions of the book and to Bill McWilliams, who heroically plowed through the entire thing at the eleventh hour, still managing to give helpful comments. Thank you to Janice Tillman, who read the whole manuscript, reading into the wee hours of the morning so I could get edits back on time. Thank you to Nancy Fitzgerald and Morehouse for taking another chance on me, and, in an odd way, thank you to Hurricane Katrina, whose devastation highlighted the urgency of many of these issues just as I was completing the manuscript.

Introduction

Moral issues are complex. Black and white are good for piano keys and children under twelve—not for the intricacies of moral behavior. If the abortion issue had an easy answer, it would have been resolved by now. It is not resolved because it is complex, and shouting that the answer is easy isn't helping. On either side. Such shouting is especially not helpful for Christians. Shouting easy answers and platitudes just makes us sound stupid—very sincerely stupid sometimes, but stupid nonetheless. I want us to grow up, face the complex problems with a complex Bible in hand, and find ways to put our society back together.

There is no template that can foresee every eventuality, no law that can ensure justice in every situation without the aid of interpretation. If so, we could dispense with courtrooms and judges and juries. Take those moral issues into the public sphere and it gets even more difficult. Where is the line between private moral decision and public legislation? Can the government order me to make certain moral choices? The religious response to moral issues is more complicated still. The complete will and nature of God are beyond human understanding, yet people of faith have made a covenant to imitate that nature and follow that will in both public and private life.

The impulse for this book came from the 2004 presidential election, when everyone was talking about "moral values" as if they were cut and dried, black and white, and easy to legislate. On both the left and the right there seemed to be a shallowness in our thinking that wasn't serving either God or the public good.

The religious language covering the airwaves, especially the language coming from Christians, was becoming more and more frightening. Not because the people speaking were bad people, but because simplistic answers to complex problems can ruin the fabric of our nation, just as solving poverty by simply printing more money would ruin our economy. Describing the will of God as if God were nicely contained in a museum display, where we could see all sides and know all there was to know, was not faith but idolatry. I became afraid for both my nation and my Church. And I was angry.

So my first impulse in writing a book was to rail against my sense of having my faith co-opted by those who were broadcasting to the world that Christian faith meant an alignment with certain political and social agendas that I didn't think it stood for at all. And then to rail against my own party for steadfastly refusing to play on the faith ball field and listen to the Christian voice within the Democratic Party. But then I thought about it a little more.

The world, it seemed to me, didn't need another angry book, and Christians didn't need yet another point of division. What seemed to be lacking was real dialogue. We had a lot of name-calling, soul-condemning, and even violence in response to our differing stands, but there didn't seem to be much that was really seeking to find common ground.

More than that, there didn't seem to be much written on Christian ethics that was really accessible to those without specialized training or vocabulary. What was needed, I thought, was a book that could lay out the issues in a down-to-earth way and present some biblical grist for the mill of discussion. But that was only part of the issue that moved me.

Another problem was the lack of awareness of the social and systemic aspects of moral behavior. Americans tend to view morality as a personal matter, and certainly there is a hugely important personal component to morality. We all saw that as Monica Lewinsky's name began to dominate headlines. What troubled me in the dialogue about Bill Clinton's adultery, however, was the seeming lack of recognition that, while personal moral behavior was lacking, Clinton did pretty well in many areas of social morality. I appreciated his willingness to take on the tobacco industry, his work toward a healthier environment, and his concern for the poor. Those too are moral issues.

Then came the Bush years, when many of us see flagrant violations of social morality. But the dialogue still seems to focus on personal choices, even when the desparate faces of the New Orleans Convention

Center plead for our help in eradicating poverty and racism. When the exit pollsters in the 2004 presidential election asked me whether I voted the way I did because of "moral values," my answer was an unequivocal "yes." But it wasn't homosexuality or abortion that made me cast my vote for John Kerry. The moral issue that concerned me most was what I believe to be an unjust war in Iraq and policies that favor the rich at the expense of the poor. Bush shouldn't get a free pass from Christians just because he got sober and stayed faithful to Laura, and Clinton's morality shouldn't be judged solely on the basis of Monica Lewinsky. There's a bigger picture.

And so I wanted to write a book to remind the Christians among us that Christian faith and moral behavior have more than just a personal dimension. As a United Methodist, this is part of my faith heritage. The combination of personal holiness and social justice is a hallmark of John Wesley's theology, and it was more than evident in his life. Some have said that the reason England did not have the violent social unrest that France endured during the French Revolution was because the Wesleys managed to convince England that morality had a social dimension.

The Wesleyan movement reformed prisons, built orphanages, started women's work co-operatives, and traveled from house to house delivering food to the poor. Wesleyans took the message of personal responsibility out to the streets where the people gathered, even as they held the rich accountable for the social and political structures that often made such personal responsibility by the poor impossible. It is time for such a call again.

Back to Basics

It's hard to get more basic, in terms of biblical ethics, than the Ten Commandments (which have managed to become a moral issue all by themselves), so I decided to use them as a framework to look at the various controversies that face us. Probably my own biases show in my placement of issues, but I've tried to be fair in disclosing my own positions.

The topics I deal with in these pages may surprise you. All the commandments have a personal dimension, and there are many books and sermons that can help us think through the day-to-day decisions we make in our personal lives. But we don't often recognize the larger picture. I can live out my personal morality only so far before I start running into social structures and governmental systems that have gone unchecked for so long that they now prevent the type of personal morality that they once hoped to encourage.

Here's an example: I can go only so far in trying to make one out of every seven days a day of Sabbath rest. Sooner or later (a time frame largely dependent on my income) I run into our 24/7 culture that demands constant work and constant economic exchange. Systems outside of myself have made my personal desire to keep the fourth commandment impossible.

I can be very intentional about not killing, but the more serious I become about keeping this commandment, the more I run into things like the taxes I pay that support capital punishment (which I oppose) and a war I consider unjust. I may not kill anyone directly, but my tax dollars pay for others to do so. You may disagree with my position, but the point is that I am prevented from living what I consider to be a moral life because of restrictions from the outside. I can be a conscientious objector if I'm drafted, but to my knowledge the IRS has no such designation.

I have strong personal moral values, but when I really try to live them out, I discover that there are huge national, and sometimes global, systems that prevent me from doing what I believe is right. This is a book primarily about those systems and issues—the public and social face of moral behavior.

The Foundation

The Ten Commandments are actually listed twice in the Bible: in Exodus 20:1–17 and Deuteronomy 5:6–21. There are slight differences, which I will highlight as we go along, but basically they are the same listing. Different traditions, however, look at them in different ways, starting with the numbering system.

Exodus 34:28 calls them the *Ten* Commandments, so most numbering systems work with that, even though there are more than ten commands within the text. Complicating the numbering process is the fact that the Hebrew doesn't actually say the ten "commandments," but rather the ten "words." So, for example, "I am the Lord your God who brought you out of the land of Egypt" in Exodus 20:1 is seen by the Jews as the first "word," even though it is not technically a commandment.

Even within the Christian tradition there are different numbering systems. The Roman Catholics, for example, lump the commandments about no other gods and graven images together and then split up the coveting commandment into two: the coveting of people and the coveting of property. What I am using here is the system commonly used in Protestant circles, which lays them out (in shortened form) this way. This text is from the King James Version.

1. Thou shalt have no other gods before me.
2. Thou shalt not make unto thee any graven image.
3. Thou shalt not take the name of the Lord thy God in vain.
4. Remember the Sabbath day, to keep it holy.
5. Honour thy father and thy mother.
6. Thou shalt not kill.
7. Thou shalt not commit adultery.
8. Thou shalt not steal.
9. Thou shalt not bear false witness against thy neighbor.
10. Thou shalt not covet.

I have tried to group the issues that face us under the commandment that seemed to give the most support for the discussion, although in most cases a topic could have found a home under the banner of several different commandments. I've also steered most of the discussions toward a public rather than a private application. For example, the false witness commandment can spur all sorts of discussions about whether an individual should ever tell a lie. I'll leave those questions for another time. In this book, I'm looking at the way we lie in our public life together . . . through institutions, policies, and public behavior.

Even so, the purpose of this book isn't to make public policy recommendations. This is a book by an American Christian for American Christians, to help us keep our political/social positions and our faith in responsible dialogue.

While we'll look at Church/state issues in a later chapter, I believe that a person's faith should influence whether and how a person votes on political and social matters. Christian faith is a way of living, not an activity restricted to certain days or situations. My faith has been misguided at times, but it's the guiding principle for my entire life, and it affects every choice I make, personal or political.

The Bible, in both Old and New Testaments, is clear about that. God didn't give commandments only about worship services or private life. God gave commandments about how to live together in society, in the public sphere. That's the larger meaning of politics—the word itself comes from the Greek word "polis," which means "city." "Politics" actually means the art of living together in community. Getting rid of politics is not the answer, for that would mean getting rid of community.

Although I recognize the truth of Henri Nouwen's statement that "community is where the person you least want to live with always lives," the Bible seems clear that we are not put on this earth to be lone rangers. Venturing out from our isolated caves, into the polis, into politics, is part of the Christian calling to love our neighbor. Not just the neighbor who's part of the same political party, but the neighbor identified in Luke 10:29. Who is it? A Samaritan. The enemy. The heretic. The one with racially mixed blood. The Republican. The Democrat. Even the one who voted for Ralph Nader.[1]

There is not now and has never been only one Christian way to interpret biblical texts or only one way a Christian can vote on a particular issue. A given church or denomination might have specific positions and demand that its adherents vote consistently with those. In the issues surrounding the 2004 election, both John Kerry as a Roman Catholic and George W. Bush as a United Methodist ran afoul of their respective church positions—Kerry by supporting abortion and Bush by engaging in what United Methodists consider an unjust war and supporting capital punishment.

We can say that Kerry was not being a good Catholic and that Bush wasn't being a good United Methodist. But it isn't helpful to say that either one was not being Christian. We all struggle to interpret God's word and God's will through the imperfect lens of our own lives and understanding.

It's up to each of us, in conversation with the churches and faith communities to which we belong, to enter into our own relationship with God, to consider God's revelation to us both in Scripture and in the Word made Flesh, and to decide for ourselves how we'll live and how we'll vote. Our eternal salvation isn't determined at the ballot box, and the sooner Christians quit condemning one another to hell for voting in certain ways, the quicker we'll have meaningful dialogue and come to some common ground.

This is a book meant to help Christians think and talk about the issues debated in the public sphere—and to highlight issues that Christians mostly ignore—from the perspective of Christian faith. Obviously, in the space of one book and bucket-loads of moral issues, I'm only scratching the surface—I've provided a suggested reading list through which the topics mentioned can be examined in more detail and depth. These chapters are meant as discussion starters, not conclusions . . . even though I've obviously drawn some conclusions myself.

Lastly, it needs to be said that I'm not writing this book because I'm above any moral flaws or because I've got it all figured out. Like everybody else, I have moral inconsistencies in my life. You'll see some in these pages. Some of the positions I hold today on moral issues represent a complete reversal from positions I've held at other points in my life. And it may well be that twenty years from now I'll write stridently against positions I now hold dear. We learn and grow and change through life. I found the 2004 election discussions of Kerry's supposed "flip-flops" quite strange. I appreciate a leader who can change and adapt, grow and learn as new facts come to light and as the world situation shifts. A "don't bother me with the facts" attitude seems problematic. But that's just me.

In the end, this is just an invitation to some honest, Bible-based wrestling with the issues that face us all. If you don't like my conclusions and interpretations, draw your own. The purpose is less to say, "This is right," than to say, "Let's talk." Let's quit condemning one another. Let's remember that Jesus called us to humility and service and repentance. Let's be honest about whether our dearly held positions on social issues come from the Bible or from some of our own life's baggage and fears. Let's talk about the differences between the letter of the law and the spirit of the law when it comes to Scripture. While we won't all agree even so—that would be boring anyway—maybe there will be a little more grace in our conversation, and a little more healing for our land.

1

No Other Gods

Thou shalt have no other gods before me.

Heading the list of the Ten Commandments is the command to make Yahweh the top priority. It's not an accident that this one is first. I think this one heads the list because, like the top button on a shirt, if you don't get this one right, all the rest will be messed up as well. This is the commandment about priorities, and its placement in the list resonates with the rest of Scripture, where idolatry is the number one sin. "Love the Lord your God with all your heart, with all your soul, and with all your strength." Whether you take it from Moses in Deuteronomy 6:5 or from Jesus in the Great Commandment (Matt 22:37), the message is the same. God comes first, period.

We'll talk more about this when we get to graven images, but I think it's helpful to start out with the acknowledgment that Christians have a hard time with this. No finger pointing at the neo-pagans or practitioners of other faiths. Charity begins at home, and so do the Ten Commandments. This book isn't about what other faiths should or shouldn't be doing. This book is to help Christians look within and see if we can't do better about getting our own house in order. And the first order of business is idolatry.

The things that become idols most easily are not, in and of themselves, bad things. The danger of Christian idolatry isn't a tendency to put bad things before God. The danger is taking good, wonderful,

God-given or God-created things and giving them a greater importance than God.

There's a very easy self-test, if you want to know what has moved into the top spot in your life. Imagine that Jesus is standing directly in front of you. It's not a twist of the imagination. For the sake of the test, imagine that you can be absolutely sure that this is Jesus and that God is giving you a commandment. Jesus stands there and says, "I want you to give up something, and I'll come back tomorrow to tell you what it is." Your mind starts to race in the next twenty-four hours, and I'm guessing that there are some things that you would willingly let go.

But then there would be other things—things that, if Jesus named them, you'd argue and justify and beg to keep. In fact, there may be something that Jesus could ask that you would actually refuse to give up … that you just can't see that you could live without. That thing (or person) which, in its proper place, is one of God's greatest blessings, has now become the god of your life—the thing that you'd do anything to keep, the thing that you'd protect at all costs, the thing you'd deny your faith rather than abandon. It is your god.

We see this played out in the New Testament story of the Rich Young Ruler. A rich young man comes to see Jesus and asks what he needs to do to inherit eternal life. Jesus tells him simply to keep the commandments, referring to the Ten. The young man makes the amazing claim that he's done just that since his youth. Jesus, with incredible insight, puts that claim to the test. He starts with the very first commandment, to see if there is any god that this young man has put above Yahweh. "You lack one thing," says Jesus. "Go and sell all that you have and give to the poor. Then come and follow me." Ouch!

Jesus has just stepped on the young man's god. He considers the request, hangs his head, and walks away sad. He cannot do it. Not only can he not do what Jesus asks, he realizes that he has *not* kept all the commandments since his youth. He hasn't even kept the first one. He has put his wealth before God.

On the successful front we have the story in Genesis 22:1–18 of Abraham and the binding of Isaac. In every Bible study I've ever taught, participants rise up with one voice to condemn this story. How could God ask Abraham to consider sacrificing his son? What sort of bloodthirsty God is this? It ranks in many minds as one of the most monstrous tales of Scripture.

I've never felt that way about it. To me, it's an illustration of what complete and total faith in God looks like. Abraham loves his son, both because Isaac is his family and because this child represents God's promise. Isaac is the child that Abraham and Sarah were never supposed to be able to have. He's the miracle baby, the son of the promise, and the object of their joy and adoration. And yet, with heavy steps, he climbs Mt. Moriah to do the unthinkable because the one being who was more important to Abraham than Isaac has asked him to.

The root question of this story (which is helping us to see why Abraham was chosen of all the people on the earth to introduce God to the world) is whether Abraham has any other gods before Yahweh. There is no question that it's the ultimate test. With Isaac gone, no amount of the Rich Young Ruler's wealth would have made any difference. Isaac was all. If anything could stand in the way of Abraham following God's will, Isaac would be that thing. And so Abraham's allegiance is tested. He passes the test and retains both his faith and his son. God doesn't want child sacrifice. God wants our ultimate allegiance.

I'm not saying any of this is easy. I'm just trying to get us to begin at a place of honesty. Even without putting Abraham's horrible choice into the equation, most of us have other gods that get our attention more readily than the God of Jesus Christ. I know in my own life I've lost it the minute Jesus shows up and says, "Hand over your computer!" Never mind family or friends or job or reputation, I'm knocked out of the running by my hard drive. Thank God for the gospel of grace.

In any case, what we do on a personal level, we also do in our public life. By "we," I mean Christians. Of course there are plenty of others who do this as well, but this is not a book about them. This is a book about us—about the things we do, and whether we, as Christians ought to keep doing them.

The Bottom Line

The business world is as good a place to start as any, as it is full of gods that compete for our public attention. St. Anselm defined God as "a being than which no greater can be conceived." To see what god runs a business, I would alter that definition just slightly and say that the god of a particular enterprise is "a *good* than which no greater can be conceived." We think of God as being at the top, but in business we define "good" at the bottom. It is the bottom line—the "good" for which every aspect of a business is designed.

I don't believe it was always so, but it seems that in twenty-first century America, the bottom line of most businesses is profit. In 2004 I went to a management seminar. With a growing staff at the church I was serving, I knew I needed some additional skills and believed that the business world could help me out. So I signed up and went to a day-long seminar, run by a nationwide secular company that provides such training. There were a lot of helpful tips I picked up during the day, and then we gathered for some closing remarks from a retired executive of a large automaker.

"So, why do we do all this?" he asked. "Why should we work to be better managers and improve the companies for which we work?" It was a good question, and I waited for the profound answer. I swear I am not making this up. "We do all of this," he declared with confidence, "so that we can get more toys. With better management comes bigger profits and therefore bigger salaries. With bigger salaries you can get the better car, the larger home, and all the other things you want right now that you can't afford."

I about came out of my chair, and the other church staff member who went with me had to beg me not to create a scene. I waited for the man to say he was kidding. He never did. That's what it was all about . . . the toys . . . the salary . . . the profit. I didn't cause a scene, but I did speak to the man afterward, telling him that some of us had goals beyond profit, and that what he had just taught was making my job as a minister ever so much harder because too many people in the country believed him.

The bottom line of profit and larger salaries is killing our country. While people here are unemployed, jobs are exported to cheap labor markets. Those who have jobs are often overworked because a business is unwilling to cut into profits to pay enough workers to do the job. If costs need to be cut, they are not cut from the salaries of top executives; the jobs of workers further down the line disappear. The television ads would lead you to believe that the bottom line of a business is the service they provide. For some that is true. I don't believe it is true for most. Most cannot conceive of a greater good than profit. It is their god.

The issue for the Christian is to identify the god of the place where we are employed and then determine whether that god is a manifestation of the God of Jesus Christ. What we do for a living is not immaterial to Christian life. The early Christians knew this and there were certain jobs that the first-century church forbade Christians to hold. Eberhard Arnold in *The Early Christians in Their Own Words* writes,

> The rank afforded by property and profession was recognized to be incompatible with [Christian] fellowship and simplicity, and repugnant to it. For that reason alone, the early Christians had an aversion to any high judicial position and commissions in the army. They found it impossible to take responsibility for any penalty or imprisonment, any disfranchisement, any judgment over life or death, or the execution of any death sentence pronounced by martial or criminal courts. Other trades and professions were out of the question because they were connected with idolatry or immorality. Christians therefore had to be prepared to give up their occupations. The resulting threat of hunger was no less frightening than violent death by martyrdom.[1]

Christians today need to ask themselves whether they are worshipping another god through their employer. Is your labor being used to support systems of injustice that harm the poor? That exploit the earth? That value profit over people? The question of a Christian's employment is a far-reaching one, and one with no small economic cost to Christian families. We don't want to look at it, because we're afraid of what we'll find. But it's the question of the first commandment and the choice Joshua once put so clearly to the Hebrews as they were poised to enter the Promised Land: "Choose you this day whom you will serve" (Josh 24:15). Christian faith requires great courage.

The National Interest

"If we have to use force, it is because we are America. We are the indispensable nation. We stand tall. We see further into the future."
   —Secretary of State Madelaine Albright, NBC Today Show,
      February 19, 1998.

"America must prevent other states from challenging our leadership or seeking to overturn the established political and economic order... We must maintain the mechanisms for deterring potential competitors from even aspiring to a larger regional or global role."
   —Pentagons' Defense Planning Guide for 1994–1999.

Related to the bottom line of a business and to "the good than which no greater can be conceived," is the bottom line and greatest good for a nation. The political language asks whether something is "in our national interest." In and of itself, the national interest is not a bad thing. Nations ought to ask that question, just as individuals ought to question whether a particular action shows respect and love for themselves and their families.

The tricky part comes when the national interest comes into conflict with either the common good or behavior forbidden or mandated for Christians. Again, I'm not trying to say that the Christian ethic must be imposed on a nation. But I am trying to say that when a Christian is making a decision on participation in the work of a government, the first commandment directs us to ask whether we are being asked to swear our primary allegiance to another god. I am also trying to say that we should be careful about claiming that our nation behaves in anything like a Christian fashion.

For four years, James A. Joseph was the United States ambassador to Nelson Mandela's South Africa. On June 29, 2004, Ambassador Joseph gave a lecture at the Chautauqua Institute on Ethics and Diplomacy. It was a fine lecture and made some excellent points, but the thing that really dropped my jaw wasn't the body of the lecture but the introduction.

Ambassador Joseph said he wanted to talk about ethics and diplomacy, "to ask whether the marriage of these two concepts is a conceptual contradiction that has no place in the real politick of the modern world as some claim or can there be principled diplomacy that considers both what is right and what is in the national interest?"[2] Okay, I thought, let me get this straight. Our former ambassador to South Africa is giving a prestigious lecture in order to raise the question of whether "ethical diplomacy" is an oxymoron. What?

I listened some more. "It is true that heads of state and the diplomats who represent them are expected to ask, first, in any transaction what is in the national interest, but Nelson Mandela often baffled his own diplomats, not to mention those from other countries, by asking what is right."[3] An ugly door opened. Silly me. Here I was thinking that diplomats were out there seeking the good of the world. But no. Apparently the unwritten rule of diplomacy is to get the other nations to do whatever your nation wants, even if it might ruin them in the process. Nelson Mandela rose above that to seek the good of all, and people were "baffled."

That says a lot as well. It wasn't that people were mad or surprised or disappointed. They were baffled by someone sitting at the diplomacy table asking for moral behavior. They didn't get it. Diplomacy that considered the welfare of any other state was completely outside their understanding. It was like an ant contemplating algebra (or me contemplating algebra, for that matter). They were baffled by the entry of ethics into diplomacy.

What does it mean, for a country that loves to put flags in our churches, that our diplomats are completely baffled when they encounter ethical behavior? I'm sure lots of people will write to me to tell me about ethical diplomats they have known. I know there are some, Ambassador Joseph among them. But the presentation of a lecture at the Chautauqua Institute asking whether it is even permissible to put ethics and diplomacy in the same sentence makes me think that ethical diplomacy isn't a widespread practice.

That it isn't common can be seen in some of the descriptions of Mandela's behavior. Joseph writes that Mandela "was optimistic that he could penetrate the worst instinct of his adversaries because, while working to change their policies and practices, he demonstrated a respect for their humanity, an understanding of their traditions and sensitivity to the demands of their culture."[4] Even a casual glance at our response to 9/11 shows that we did nothing of the kind with our adversaries, going so far in the other direction that we ended up with the revolting hell that was Abu Ghraib.

Joseph also reports that Mandela "required potential investors to show what value, what social good, would be added by their presence."[5] Oh my. I may be naïve about some things, but you can't convince me that we evaluate potential investors in the U.S. by anything other than their potential to boost our economy. Imagine what our country would look like if we started insisting that a corporation prove that a social, and not just an economic, good would result from their presence.

Suppose even a single city asked that question of businesses that wanted to build there. Suppose the mayor said, "I know you'll bring lots of money to the city, but you're a big polluter and you'll demoralize our small, family-owned businesses. You can't come in." Suppose the town council said, "Yes, it would bring lots of jobs with higher incomes. But your type of business is proven to increase crime and corruption in its surrounding area. You can't come in."

I know there are groups of Christian business owners in this country. I know there are Christian politicians—not just the ones who wave Bibles, but the ones who are actually in the pews of churches trying to live a Christian life. And we are successful in some areas. Christians often stand up and oppose casinos and sometimes liquor establishments. But again, those things focus the effects on personal morality. How about the polluters or those who exploit foreign labor and illegal immigrants? We've taken some steps, but we can do more.

Why aren't we lobbying for greater ethical focus in diplomacy? Why is the public face of Christian diplomacy Pat Robertson calling for the assassination of the democratically elected President of Venezuela? If a secular government official had said that, he would be out of a job. Why is Pat Robertson still supported by Christians?

Freedom

My father's family goes back to the 1700s in New Hampshire. The state's motto, as emblazoned on the license plates, is "Live Free or Die," a statement written by Revolutionary War hero General John Stark on July 31, 1809. Part of living free in New Hampshire means not having laws that some other states take for granted, like requiring the driver of a car to wear a seat belt or the driver of a motorcycle to wear a helmet. Looking at that sometimes makes me think that "Live Free *and* Die" would be a more appropriate motto. But residents of New Hampshire don't want to be bound by any state laws telling them what they can and cannot do.

At least in popular rhetoric, freedom is the primary value in the United States. "They hate freedom" has been a line I've heard a number of times from those who want to label another individual or group as an enemy of American values. And, as values go, I don't think a secular nation could select a better one. In fact, in my reading of the Bible, human freedom seems to be God's primary value as well. It seems to be the one thing that God will not violate, from the minute that God gave Adam and Eve the freedom to eat of the forbidden fruit to the moment God allowed human beings to nail Jesus to a cross. We are called to love, and love must be free. If you ask me, there's exactly one human right, and freedom is it.

But even freedom, that blessed gift that more than all others allows us to experience God, can become an idol. It can cease to be the means to know God—and knock God off the throne instead. First John 4:8 claims that "God is love." When freedom tramples love, it has become an idol.

Gun Control

My first instinct was to put the issue of gun control into the "Thou shalt not kill" chapter. But as I thought about it, that was too biased toward my own view. Most of the debate about gun control isn't about killing. It's about freedom and the meaning of the Second Amendment to the Constitution, which reads: "A well regulated Militia being necessary to the security of a free State, the right of the people to keep and bear Arms shall not be infringed."

I'll be honest. I don't like guns. I don't recall that I've ever even held a gun in my hands, let alone shot one, and if a genie were to grant me three wishes, I think I would use one of them to undo the invention of the gun. Their purpose is to kill and I don't like killing. So, personally, I'm all for gun abolition rather than gun control.

But I know that's not where most people are, and it's probably not very smart. It also isn't very supportive of the Second Amendment. But I've found the policies lobbied for by the NRA and other gun advocates to be as ridiculously extreme on the other end of the spectrum and just as neglectful of the Second Amendment. Why don't I hear more talk about the first phrase of the amendment, "A well regulated Militia"?

The reason the Constitution allows citizens to keep and bear arms is not because anybody should have the right to shoot doves out of the sky or to take out a burglar. It's a check against governments that become tyrannical, giving citizens the right to form their own militia to fight a government run amok. In this day and age, having the right to form private militias seems pretty scary, especially as we wage wars to rout them out of other nations. What's the difference between an armed militia and an armed gang or a terrorist organization? Only the object of their wrath, which is a subjective thing indeed.

That's where the "well regulated" part comes in. I'm not a constitutional scholar, but it seems to me that the regulation of arms is part of the mandate of the Second Amendment. Child-safety locks and background checks before gun purchases are part of ensuring a "well regulated Militia." While I was serving my first church, a woman showed up on my doorstep with her baby. She had run from her home after her husband had pushed her, while she was carrying the baby, down the stairs. Her sin? Objecting to the fact that her husband had spent his entire $1700 paycheck on guns, leaving nothing for rent, utility bills, or food.

That guy is within the law (except for the assault), but not within the bounds of the "well regulated Militia" protected by the Second Amendment. He is a gun-worshipping thug and he is not alone. When freedom to do what I want overrides love of neighbor, it has become an idol. I think the gun lobby crossed that line long ago. Christians interested in living the Ten Commandments (including Christians who play Moses receiving the Ten Commandments in movies) should be paying attention.

Hate speech

We do the same thing in bending over backward to protect hate speech. Christians have some pretty strong feelings about words. We believe that God created the universe through speech. "God said . . . and there was . . ." We believe that word can become flesh and live among us. So we ought to be very wary of the way speech is used in our public life.

We do get worried about sexual speech, just as we get all worked up over sexual sins. And that shouldn't be disregarded. But it's not the only harmful speech or sin on the planet, and I would argue that hate speech and hate crimes are more dangerous to society. Adultery, for example, is an individual act done in secret. In most cases adulterers do not claim righteousness or try to convince others to do the same. That doesn't make it good, but it does limit its effects. Hate speech, on the other hand, is designed to be broadcast to the public, propagated wherever possible, and targets entire demographic groups. That we give it free rein in our country is frightening.

I know that limiting speech in any way can be a slippery slope, but that's why we have law schools and legal experts and constitutional scholars to help us craft laws that protect our right to be free from at least the most blatant, hate-mongering forms of the spoken word. The line may be hard to find, but it's hard to find in laws about killing as well (is it manslaughter, self-defense, first degree, or some other?), and that doesn't stop us from making laws about that.

Christians should be very concerned about hate speech, and most especially about churches and religious institutions that practice it. It's bad enough when hate speech comes from the secular world. When it comes from those that claim to represent the Church, it is blasphemy. Our God-given right to freedom includes the right to be free from verbal intimidation and abuse. We regulate speech that can be considered sexual harassment. It's tricky, but we do it—and we should. But it's time to cast our gaze further than our sexually fixated navel and find a way to protect the larger freedoms of peace and joy by removing the virulent hate speech in our midst.

Pledge of Allegiance

On September 14, 2005, U.S. District Judge Lawrence Karlton ruled that the recitation of the Pledge of Allegiance in public schools is unconstitutional because it violates school children's right to be "free from a coercive requirement to affirm God." Perhaps by the time you read this the Supreme Court will have ruled on the issue, or perhaps it will still be waiting to be resolved.

But however the Court rules, the continued battle over prayer in school (long after it's been resolved in the courts) is an indicator that the controversy over the pledge is not likely to slink quietly away. To look at the media, you'd think that all Christians stand united under God on this one, and the fact that the case is being brought by an avowed atheist doesn't help that impression any. But it's a false one. This is an issue on which good Christians have differences, and those differences revolve around who gets our ultimate allegiance. For many, it's a first-commandment issue.

First, some basic history. The pledge was written in 1892 by a Baptist minister and socialist named Francis Bellamy, and was published a few months later in a children's magazine on the occasion of the four-hundredth anniversary of the arrival of Columbus in the Americas. It read, "I pledge allegiance to my Flag and the Republic for which it stands, one nation, indivisible, with liberty and justice for all."[6]

Although composed by a minister, there was no "under God" in the pledge until the nation started to get worried about the atheists of Soviet communism in McCarthy's 1950s. The Knights of Columbus started the movement to have the words "under God" inserted into the pledge, but it took the Rev. George Docherty to really get the ball rolling. With President Eisenhower sitting in the pews, Rev. Docherty preached a sermon pointing out that the pledge of allegiance to the United States could easily be said by any little child in Moscow—that there was no difference between them and us. That did it. Congress inserted "under God" into the pledge in 1954 and it was signed into law on Flag Day that year, despite the fact that Bellamy's son and grandchildren wrote to Congress to object. Bellamy would not have wanted that insertion, they insisted.[7]

Why would a Christian minister object? Well, going back to his Baptist roots, Bellamy would have been a staunch supporter of the separation of Church and state. The Baptists began in America in my home state of Rhode Island, founded by Roger Williams, who fled there when the Massachusetts Bay Colony wanted to make a Puritan out of him. He didn't want a state-sponsored religion. He wanted religious freedom. So Williams left Massachusetts (and the Puritans, who had left Britain for exactly the same reason) and went south, creating a state where the government could not dictate what he could or couldn't believe. Rhode Island is home to both the first Baptist church and the first Jewish synagogue in America.

Many who want to take "under God" out of the pledge fear that the specter of state-sponsored religion is hovering again—that the nation founded on a principle of religious liberty is creating its own religious tyranny. We've known that atheists feel this way, but it's not often pointed out that many Christians, like Bellamy, don't want that phrase in the pledge either—not because we don't believe in God, but because we're keenly aware of the dangers of confusing God and country.

Even before the "under God" phrase was inserted, some refused to recite the pledge on religious grounds. Some Mennonites and Quakers, and all Jehovah's Witnesses, feel that to pledge allegiance to anything other than God is a violation of the first commandment to have no other gods. For the same reason there are many pastors who squirm at the sight of the American flag in the church. They don't hate America, they just don't want to have any confusion between the word of God and the word of Congress. Many from the Vietnam era have the same sort of wariness.

On the first anniversary of the September 11th attacks, many of us had services to recognize the occasion. As I prepared my sermon in early September 2002, it was obvious from the rhetoric coming out of Washington that we were going to attack Iraq. A pre-emptive strike on a sovereign country that had not attacked us or our allies or anybody outside of its borders seemed to me to go against everything I believed as a Christian and every principle I thought America stood for. But I could see and hear plainly that it was coming—no matter what anybody thought, no matter what the U.N. said, no matter what weapons the inspectors found (or didn't find).

And so, on the Sunday closest to the anniversary I made what is probably the most inflammatory remark of my ministry to date. I said, "To my mind, when the first pre-emptive bomb falls on Iraq, we may as well take the line out of the pledge of allegiance. We will no longer be 'one nation, under God.'" Reaction was extreme. Some people brought me presents. Others threatened to leave the church.

When Christians are uncomfortable with "under God" in the pledge, that's the sort of thing we're talking about. If God starts sleeping with Country, the offspring claim both divine and secular authority. For me, it's bad enough that my country is running around bombing other nations at will, but it adds insult to injury to proclaim to the world that God is behind it. Some people may believe God endorses such things, and they have a right to believe that. But don't force such beliefs on me by implying that whatever my country does is under God's will. The phrase "under God" doesn't explicitly do that, but for me it comes a bit too close for comfort.

The current political atmosphere is so saturated with religious language and association that I no longer feel free, even as a Christian minister. When I express political dissent, people call both my patriotism and my faith into question. Those two things are not supposed to go together. A dear friend of mine, now a United States citizen, defected from communist Czechoslovakia in the early 1980s. She said to me, "I feel less free to voice my opinion now than I did under the communists. There, everybody knew there were dissenters and those who were with the party. Dissent was not accepted by the government, but it was perfectly accepted among friends and with the people. Here, you cannot oppose government action in any circle at all without feeling threatened or intimidated."

I can't speak to what it was like living under communism, but I can say that I agree with her fears about voicing opposition to government policy and practice in the here and now, and it seems to me that we've gotten to that point because we confused our nation and its Christ-professing president with God.

But then, to take up the other side for a moment, it could be instructive if we really emphasized that we were "UNDER God." Most of the time, we seem to act as though God were under us, and our arrogance is so blatant that it must make God blush. If we truly were a nation that was submissive to God's will, even atheists might recognize the benefit and leave well enough alone.

It's ironic that it was the fear of state-sponsored atheism that got the words inserted in the first place, and now it is atheist Michael A. Newdow who is trying, out of fear of state-sponsored religion, to remove them. The failure and abuses of communism, the failure and abuses of the Taliban, and the failure and abuses of the Holy Roman Empire all ought to tell us that government should quit meddling in religion. Don't endorse it, but don't prevent it either. The battles in the United States seem dangerously close to both mistakes, and the fears that result on both sides are doing us harm.

No, we shouldn't force kids to pray in public schools, but neither should we say that an empty school building can't be voluntarily used by people who choose to pray or that a child can't express personal faith with a prayer or religious adornment. Given the way that some groups use religion as a front for hate groups, what people actually say in those prayers or show in that adornment should be taken into consideration, but religious expression shouldn't be barred from the public sphere any more than it should be mandated.

Some people want to eliminate the inaugural prayer for new presidents. That seems silly to me. An inaugural celebration is about the president. If the president wants to have a prayer at the inaugural, then there should be a prayer that reflects his or her beliefs. If we elect an atheist, that person should be free to dispense with a prayer. Why is that so difficult?

There are many, many gods both in our personal lives and in our culture. In their proper place, they are great blessings, gifts given to us by God in trust, in trust that we won't worship them and forget our first love. The danger is not that we love our country, but that we love our country more than God. The danger is not that we value freedom, but that we put our personal freedoms above God's will. The danger is not that we want to make a profit from our labor, but that profit becomes the thing for which we will make ultimate sacrifices. This is a commandment about the centrality of God. It is the hardest commandment to keep, but the rewards for doing so spread from ourselves to the world.

2

No Graven Images

*Thou shalt not make unto thee any graven image,
or any likeness of any thing that is in heaven above,
or that is in the earth beneath, or that is in the
water under the earth: Thou shalt not bow down
thyself to them, nor serve them: for I the Lord thy
God am a jealous God, visiting the iniquity of the
fathers upon the children unto the third and fourth
generation of them that hate me; and shewing
mercy unto thousands of them that love me, and
keep my commandments.*

I think this commandment may win the prize for causing the most grief and devastation. In the summer of 2004, I spent about a month and a half in Scotland, tending a Methodist congregation and touring as far as my little rental Peugeot would take me.

Being a pastor, I tended to seek out the religious sites, especially cathedrals and abbeys. Some had been refurbished, at least in part, but almost all had seen ruin during the years of the Scottish Reformation. With the fervent zeal of John Knox interpreting the commandment against graven images to mean any religious sculpture, carving, or painting, the world of religious art experienced its Armageddon in the mid-sixteenth century.

At Rosslyn Chapel I saw the painstaking renovation work being done to save the intricate carvings that the Reformation had left open to wind and air. Rosslyn was one of many Scottish houses of worship where Oliver Cromwell decided to stable his horses. All the original statues there were destroyed.

I remember looking at a bas relief above an arched doorway at the ruined Melrose Abbey that Sir Walter Scott loved so well. The archway was rimmed with figures; you could see their flowing robes. Who were they? Disciples? Saints? We don't know. The reformers chopped off all their heads. The ruined walls of every abbey and cathedral have similar stories to tell.

The commandment about graven images is concerned with idolatry. The Hebrew word *pecel* refers very specifically to carved images, but that is by no means the only sort of image worried about in Scripture. A repetition of the prohibition in Leviticus 26:1 describes other types of images, both concrete and abstract, that might come to be worshiped in God's place.

When this commandment was given, adherents of the religions that the Hebrews encountered worshipped images carved of stone, wood, or other materials. And those carved images weren't just spiritual aids to help people connect with a god who was elsewhere. They actually believed that bit of stone or wood was the god itself.

But the worship of Yahweh, the prophets insisted, was to be different. God wanted no confusion: Yahweh could not be contained in a branch of wood or a chunk of stone. This was a living God, not subject to the manipulation of human hands. The concern of the commandment is that people not carve God in stone and that the Israelites not limit their God to a particular location (thus a traveling tabernacle) or one kind of face, shape, or image.

At the time of the Protestant Reformation in the sixteenth century, some of the reformers took this commandment to mean that representing God in any artistic format was sinful. Certainly there is always the danger that religious art will become more important than the God it represents. In many churches in America it is heresy to suggest that Jesus looked like anything other than Warner Sallman's "Head of Christ"— that blond, light-skinned portrait that hangs or has hung in just about every church in the country.

To suggest that this famous painting gives us a glimpse of Jesus is a partial truth. To suggest that Sallman's rendering is the only representation of Jesus' appearance that is allowed is idolatry. A black Jesus, an Asian Jesus—even (gasp) a female Jesus—can also give us a tiny peek into the vast mystery of God's word becoming flesh and dwelling among us. Imagine the mess we'd be in if Jesus had come in the age of the camera or even at the height of portrait painting! The idolatry of the objects that might have been created would be almost insurmountable.

Religious art can cause difficulties. In the wake of religious questioning in response to *The DaVinci Code* by Dan Brown, I've found otherwise intelligent people who need to be reminded that DaVinci was not actually present with his canvas at the Last Supper. He painted his own truth, which may have included Mary Magdalene by Jesus' side. I've been stunned by the number of people who need to be reminded that proving that one of the disciples in the painting is really a woman is a different task than proving that a woman occupied that place at the actual event. Confusing representational art with the thing it claims to represent is a real issue, and the better the artist, the greater the danger.

That said, however, there is psychological and spiritual benefit in allowing our faith to have access to all of our senses. The tabernacle and later the Temple in Jerusalem that God instructed the people to build weren't austere and plain. Though they weren't embellished with representations of Yahweh, they were adorned with pictures of just about everything else, from the fruits of Creation to the cherubim and seraphim of the heavenly realms. And if we weren't meant to surround ourselves with beauty in worship, I don't think we'd have been given this stunning Garden Earth. God is a lover of art and the consummate artist. But God cannot be contained in any artistic expression—even God's own artistic expression in tree and lion, sea and star.

The Ten Commandments

Ironically, the Ten Commandments, which so strongly prohibit idols, have become in our day an idol themselves. Alabama judge Roy Moore captured the attention of the press when he refused a court order to remove a monument of the Ten Commandments from his courthouse. Later, the monument was taken to cities across the country, where people cheered it on and even kissed it.

I wonder if, when people get close enough to the monument to kiss it, they take the time to read commandment number two. Maybe it's just me, but it seems odd that this image of God's law, carved in stone, has become exactly the thing its words prohibit. Most of those folks might never put a St. Christopher medal in their cars, but I'd bet large sums that if the industry of religious kitsch comes up with Ten Commandments tablets to hang from a rear-view mirror, tons of saint-condemning Protestants would buy them.

You can read a general discussion of the Ten Commandments, their content, and the different ways they're counted and considered in the Introduction. But here, let's look at the controversy around their display and usage.

First let's remember first that when Moses came down the mountain with the commandments the second time (don't forget—he smashed the first edition), the commandments weren't put on permanent display. God never told Moses or anybody else to keep them visible. Perhaps they were for a time—we're not told—but once the Ark of the Covenant was built, Exodus 25:16 says that the tablets—there called the "covenant" or "testimony"—were to be stored inside it, then covered with the "mercy seat" from which Moses was to make his judgments. If they ever were removed, we're not told about it, and they disappeared when the Ark of the Covenant did.

Why wouldn't God want the tablets out for all to see and be reminded of the Law of God? Why store them in a box? Maybe God was afraid they'd become an idol. Certainly that happened to another important object from that period. Remember when God gets fed up with the Israelites' whining in the desert and sends them poisonous snakes in Numbers 21? God tells Moses to put up a bronze snake on a pole—anyone who looks at it will be cured of the snake bites. Later in Israel's history, in 2 Kings 18:4, we learn that the thing is still around, but now it has been given a name, Nehushtan, and people are bowing down to it as an idol. It had to be destroyed.

God, I think, knew our tendency to make idols—to take very good and wonderful things and elevate them above God. That would be a good reason for putting the tablets inside the ark. Moses was to make his judgments seated on top of them, for God's law was the foundation for all law. They weren't on public display so that no one would be tempted to forget that God was a living being, not to be found in tablets of stone.

Sometimes it seems that the Ten Commandments have indeed become an idol. When someone objects to their public display, people cry that God is being denied and cast out, forgetting that God and the Ten Commandments are very different things, and no human being has the power to keep God out of anywhere. Refusing to hang a plaque listing the Ten Commandments in a courtroom doesn't keep God out of that courtroom any more than putting them up brings God in.

But the controversy does reveal one thing. Refusing the Ten Commandments a public home is an example of the way our country has, in some places, become faith-phobic. The Ten Commandments were a formative part of our heritage and one of the bases for our legal system. You can honor the Christian history of a nation by displaying its symbols without adopting its faith.

Ironically, some of those same people who oppose displays of the Ten Commandments were terribly upset when the Taliban blew up huge Buddha statues in Afghanistan. Both the Taliban and those embroiled in the Ten Commandments controversy seem to think that a religious object cannot have purely historical or artistic value. Maybe they're right, but that's not the discussion I'm hearing.

I think it should be the discussion. The controversy over the Ten Commandments brings that question to the forefront. It's the same question that was answered with violent destruction of Catholic sanctuaries in Scotland and other places. Can religious art ever be just art? Museums seem to think so. But moving that art into our living, worshiping, and public spaces seems to muddy the waters. So, first, let's think about why God didn't command Moses to display them.

Second, let's remember that these sayings are more properly called the "Ten Words" or "covenant" rather than the "Ten Commandments." These aren't commands given in a vacuum. They are words from God to God's people. They are commands only if the people accept the relationship that is offered with them. These Ten Words from God represent God's covenant with Israel. A covenant is not imposed; it is freely chosen. The commandments are binding on Israel only if they accept the offer of covenant relationship with God.

So to insist that all people be governed by the Ten Commandments regardless of whether they've chosen to accept that covenant relationship is a violation of human freedom. God didn't do it to Israel, Jesus didn't do it to his disciples, and we shouldn't do it either. Christian faith must be freely chosen, because a God who respects human freedom is part of the nature of the God revealed to us in Jesus. To violate that freedom ourselves is to proclaim a false God. Christians have done it in the past, and it has ended in atrocity.

On a personal level, I feel that seeing the Ten Commandments in a place where everyone doesn't share the faith they represent cheapens them. It feels a bit voyeuristic, like having someone put a webcam in my home to watch me pray and read and live my life so that others who have no real interest in my prayers or my books or my life can watch. The Ten Words begin with an intimate identification… "I am the Lord your God, who brought you out of the land of Egypt." The Ten Words are God's marriage proposal to Israel and, I believe, to all who call themselves the people of God. A few may want their marriage proposal broadcast on national television. Most of us, however, prefer to cherish it as an intimate moment between the lover and the beloved. It is too important and life-altering a proposal to accept merely because of peer pressure or fear of public shame.

Personally, I prefer not to see images of the Ten Commandments in public places. If you must hang them somewhere, hang them in churches so we can remember that our particular style of worship is not God, that Sabbath-keeping is a commandment, and that if we're going to call ourselves Christian, we'd better not take that name in vain. Better yet, let's engrave them underneath all of the pews, covered with a pew cushion as a mercy seat, to remind us of the covenant that is our foundation, and the need for law to be covered in mercy.

Evolution and Creationism

In the interest of full disclosure, I admit that the passions surrounding this debate baffle me. The evidence is that we have a physical world in which we live. It's a beautiful world, an intricate world, a world of interdependent systems that work to sustain life against unbelievable odds. This world and all that is in it is, simply, incredible.

The scientific community has more than enough to deal with in trying to figure out how it works—including figuring out how it got to be the way we see it today. The faith community has a different task— to ask the philosophical and religious questions about the life we see. Is what we see the ultimate truth, the ultimate answer? Is it the result of random chance occurrences, or is there a force beyond it? If there's a force beyond, what is that force like and what role did it play—or does it continue to play—in both our formation and our continued existence?

In the creation/evolution debate, I sense that both sides have violated their boundaries. I've yet to meet any human being who was present at the moment of the earth's creation. Eyewitnesses are not available. We have the witness of Scripture, inspired by the Spirit to be sure but penned nevertheless by people who weren't present and only wanted to convey the spiritual truth of the matter. Science was not their interest.

Though the first creation story in Genesis 1 presents the process in evolutionary order (the second creation story in Genesis 2 puts the order differently), the majesty of the story and the glory of the natural world leads me to the same supernatural conclusion. This world isn't random. Somebody incredibly smart and with unmatched artistic genius designed this place and gave me the honor of tending my little portion for a while.

Exactly how that incredibly smart artistic genius went about doing it doesn't concern me in the least. Whether God created a single ingeniously designed cell and tossed it into the primordial soup, watching it evolve with delight, or whether God painstakingly designed every one of some quarter million plant species by hand simply doesn't matter to me. Neither does it affect how I live out my faith.

There are three truths in the Genesis creation accounts that affect my faith and, by extension, my life. 1. God is the author. 2. It was created good. 3. Human beings were given the responsibility to tend it according to God's wishes. Science can't come into my faith and say those things aren't true—not just because I don't want them to, but because they can't. Those are not things that science can measure or determine. They're beyond the realm of what scientific method can address.

So when it comes to teaching, those in the scientific community need to present their findings on origins with humility. They can point to certain mechanics of creation and evolution—theories that may eventually be proven right or wrong—but they're not equipped to say whether God had any role, what the purpose of existence is, or whether there is any inherent goodness or spirit in it. Those things belong to the realm of faith.

At the same time, we in the faith community cannot insist that a sacred religious text solves all the questions of twenty-first-century science. I don't think Christians should prohibit the scientific community from sharing their wisdom with students. People of faith, like men and women of science, need to practice the virtue of humility.

The Christian faith ought to work hand in hand with science. Our beliefs about the author of creation tell us that God is the author of all science. When scientists tell us, "We have overwhelming evidence that the earth is more than six thousand years old," we need to re-examine our understanding with humility and grace. God speaks through geologists as well as through preachers.

We may not change our minds, but we need to be open to the discussion. Our record is not good. Remember when the Holy Office under Pope Paul V issued the opinion that the Copernican doctrine was "foolish and absurd, philosophically and formally heretical inasmuch as it expressly contradicts the doctrine of Holy Scripture in many passages . . . "? We don't need to abandon our faith because of overwhelming fossil evidence. Instead we need to keep our minds open to the amazing works of our Creator.

If both science and religion could get a good dose of humility, we might work together on these issues. If scientists hadn't become so afraid of faith (for some historically good reasons), they might see that while they can't definitively prove a theory like intelligent design, the existence of such a designer is certainly the most obvious place to start, given the evidence. And if Christians could trust a bit more in the gifts God has given to scientists, we might find our way to a deep, God-centered faith that didn't require people to leave their brains at the church door.

I have included this discussion in the chapter about graven images because I think both sides of the debate concern idolatry. We're trying to force God into our own scientific theories and biblical interpretations, then carve those ideas into unchanging stone. And whether we're talking about a living God or quantum physics, turning the dynamic to stone is the path to falsehood.

Republican or Democrat?

Another way that we try to carve God's image into an image of our making is in labeling people as either liberal or conservative, then demonizing whichever side isn't us. In the 2004 election, many people were frustrated not only by labels, but by the sealed-off entrance to a political party when a person didn't exactly fit the concrete mold of that party's platform.

For example, I know several people who were passionate about most of the traditional concerns of the Democrats, but who felt exiled because there was no room in the party for even a moderate pro-life stance on abortion. They felt driven to vote, very hesitantly, for George Bush, simply because the Democratic Party wouldn't budge on this issue. They didn't like Bush, but voted for him because the Democrats' pro-choice god was carved in stone.

I also knew a Republican who didn't like John Kerry but voted for him anyway, because the Republicans couldn't admit mistakes in Iraq.

The rightness of that war was as much an idol for the Republican Party as the pro-choice stance was for the Democrats. And those are just two of the issues.

Some people in the church that I served in 2004 came to me in frustration because their identity as Christians automatically labeled them as Republicans. They weren't. The image of a Christian as a right-leaning Republican is an image fast turning to immovable rock.

On the left is an equal and opposite injustice: the thinking that only the liberals are true to the teachings of Jesus and that the right-wing path is the road to destruction. Since the Democratic Party doesn't seem interested in reaching out to liberal Christianity (largely because they have believed the fiction that all Christians are right-wing Republicans), faithful, left-leaning Christians often feel exiled from the political sphere—and, increasingly, persecuted by it.

I've read the Bible cover to cover more times than I can count and—trust me—there are more than enough Bible passages, even within the sayings of Jesus, to make both Republicans and Democrats decidedly uncomfortable. When Jesus uses an ethnic slur and calls the Canaanites "dogs" (Matt 15:26), the politically correct left looks the other way in shame. When Jesus forgives a capital crime in John 8:11 without so much as a fine, the hawkish right turns to the Old Testament instead. There is no one "Christian" party and no one Christian way to vote; God's word provides both support and problems to both sides. To give the impression that God is limited to either Republican or Democrat, conservative, liberal, or something else entirely, is to solidify God into a particular object with specific boundaries—a graven image and an idol.

Idols always end up demanding human sacrifice, and in the case of our intense political polarization, the sacrifice has been the unity of our country. We've become afraid to speak our minds, to offer an opinion contrary to the political culture in which we travel. That sort of fear is exactly what leads to the tyranny of the majority. If we don't make up our minds to smash our political idols into dust, the future of our nation is in jeopardy.

To destroy these idols, we need a strong dose of moral courage. We need the courage to step across the aisle and say, "Some people use abortion as birth control. We need to find a way to prevent that." Or, "Guns kill lots of innocent people and it's too easy to get them and to shoot them. We need more effective controls." Who has the courage to lay their positions and their wealth on the line and admit mistakes? Who has the courage to stand up to powerful and well-heeled lobbyists? When will we stop having contests between my idol and yours and have meaningful debate?

Household Gods

When we clergy begin our ministry at a new church, one of the first things we need to do is to find out about the "household gods." It's a reference to Old Testament stories like those of Rachel, who fled her father's house with Jacob but stole the household gods (Gen 31:19) before she left. Though they belonged to the family that had formed the faith of Israel and should have been worshipping Yahweh alone, Rachel and Jacob were hedging their bets with a host of lesser deities. As they made their getaway, they packed up these little gods—probably carved in wood and stone, and easy to carry and conceal.

When clergy talk about a congregation's "household gods," we mean the way church communities worship things related to the church that aren't—in themselves—God. Like traditional idols, these household gods are usually objects. In the churches I've served, household gods have included everything from an organ, a steeple, and a garden to the pews, the flag, and the altar—even the building itself. But sometimes the gods are more abstract. I've found myself tried for heresy at the altar of favorite hymns, forms of serving communion, and clapping. And I've run afoul of gods made into the image of somebody's preferences—the ghost of someone long gone, or a person with tacit permission to block any action a church may take.

These are the household gods of a church—the things that pastors don't know are worshiped until they try to move worship in another direction, with weeping and gnashing of teeth the usual result. These household gods violate the commandment against graven images because they don't allow God to live and move. They keep Jesus sealed in the tomb of "the way we've always done it before." If these household gods can't be broken, the church will eventually become as dead as the idols it serves.

And the same sort of thing goes on in the larger political sphere. If it weren't for political dissent, we would not have the United States of America. And yet now dissenting voices are labeled as unpatriotic, even treasonous. The extreme forms of most of the debates discussed in these chapters have become the household gods of one party or the other.

They are the sacred cows that doom a candidate for straying from a political platform or for agreeing with someone from an opposing party, and they keep us from a political life that can live and breathe; grow and thrive. Of course we need to take stands and hold our positions with integrity. But when they begin to occupy the place of a god that cannot be challenged, something needs to be done.

Genetic Engineering

As genetic science is making amazing breakthroughs, religious communities have largely ignored the debate. Denominational bodies have taken official stands, but average churchgoers often have no opinion beyond what their political parties and related organizations tell them. Too often those bodies are unduly influenced by well-funded lobbyists, who are stumping for the position that will generate the most profit for their sponsors. In one way, this is understandable, as the issues are scientifically complex, but this issue is too important to allow only the voice of corporate profit to determine the outcome.

One of the most important and far-reaching issues in genetic engineering is the production of "terminator seeds"—seeds that guarantee farmers plants that are always hardy and resistant to certain pests. The trouble is they produce plants that are sterile—you can't grow a second plant from the seeds generated by the first.

Consider the implications: Farmers using terminator seeds must purchase expensive seeds every planting season, rather than harvesting seeds from the first crop to generate a second. Farmers of course are still free to buy regular seeds, but the genetic instruction that turns a regular seed into a terminator seed is spread by wind, insects, and birds. So, if the farmer down the road uses terminator seeds, his crop will alter my crop—and my plants won't produce fruitful seed.

That's tough enough for neighboring farmers to deal with. It is far more difficult when huge corporations enter the picture. Giant agricultural companies generate higher profits from terminator seeds. What is to stop them from paying farmers to plant them in areas where they could migrate to other farms?

Does this possibility seem far-fetched? Consider this true story, known as the ProdiGene incident:

> An unwanted second generation of experimental maize plants containing a protein for a pig vaccine grew in a field of soy in the U.S. Midwest.

The contamination was discovered post-harvest and resulted in about 14 million kilogrammes of soybeans being destroyed.[1]

An isolated incident? Tell that to Canadian farmer Percy Schmeiser. In 1999, Mr. Schmeiser was growing his canola crop as he had for the past forty years, using the seed from the previous year to sow the next year's crop. But a neighboring farmer had purchased genetically engineered canola seed from Missouri-based Monsanto, and it made its way into Mr. Schmeiser's crop. Not only was he faced with a crop he didn't want growing on his land, sterilizing more than 320 hectares of his canola plants, but to add insult to injury, Monsanto sued him for patent infringement, demanding that he pay a $37-per-hectare fee for this supposed theft. The case went all the way to Canada's supreme court.[2]

Monsanto, which has earned legal judgments of as much as $3 million from a single farmer, has been under investigation by the Center for Food Safety. Their 2005 review showed that Monsanto had filed ninety lawsuits against American farmers in twenty-five states, collecting more than $15 million. For these efforts, Monsanto has an annual budget of $10 million and a staff of seventy-five whose only job is investigating and prosecuting farmers. According to the above Center for Food Safety report,

> After extensive research and numerous inverviews with farmers and lawyers, CFS found that Monsanto, the world's leading agricultural biotechnology company, has used heavy-handed investigations and ruthless prosecutions that have fundamentally changed the way many American farmers farm. The result has been nothing less than an assault on the foundations of farming practices and traditions that have endured for centuries in this country and millennia around the world, including one of the oldest, the right to save and replant crop seed.[3]

The problem is huge. Though terminator seeds were banned in 1988, corporations are trying to overturn the ban, most recently at a 2005 United Nations meeting in Bangkok.[4] Also in 2005 lawmakers in Brazil approved legislation that would pave the way for the legalization of genetically modified crops, including terminator seeds.[5] Of course about 30 percent of Brazil's soy crop is already grown with genetically engineered seeds, even thought it is illegal.[6]

Is it wrong to make terminator seeds? It's tough to say for sure. I'm sure there are companies who are truly seeking to make our food supply better and farming easier through genetically modified food and seed. But Christians should ask questions and become informed enough to enter the debate. About 75 percent of processed food produced in the U.S. has been genetically modified.[7] Maybe that's a great thing, but I think it bears watching by those who profess to do justice, love mercy, and walk humbly with their God. The crop you save may be your own.

Terminator seeds are just one tiny example of the dilemmas posed by genetic engineering. When you start tampering with the human gene, the questions are infinitely more complex. What does it mean, for example, that a human gene can be patented? If you discovered the gene from cells in my body, the first one to race to the patent office with the discovery gets money from any use that gene turns out to have.[8] Is it really okay to patent and make money from human tissue? Wouldn't that stifle research and prevent the very benefit the discovery was meant to enhance? Maybe it's all fine . . . I don't know. But I do know it's not a good thing that, with the possible exception of cloning, individual Christians are not really engaged in the debate—not because there's one right answer and we're drifting away from it, but because the only voice loud enough to affect outcomes is the voice of corporate profit. Mammon has been an idol that Christians have fought and died fighting for millennia. Mammon will not make moral choices. Christians need to be engaged on behalf of our God.

The ability to alter the genetic structures of plant and animal life is astounding, giving us the power to mold life into the image of our choosing. But unchecked power can lead to astounding evil. The splitting of the atom gave us the ability to power a city or to destroy it. Christians shouldn't sit idly by and hope those making the decision will make an ethical choice.

I'm not against biotechnology. Too often Christians have feared scientific discovery and simply tried to shut it down. To make an image of God that can't include scientific advancement is creating an idol as surely as the scientist marching forward with a scientific application without regard for its ethical implications. As our scientific expertise grows by leaps and bounds, we must be careful not to take the Creator's role for ourselves, molding life according to our desires. As smart as we are, there is still too much we don't know. The science of genetics can quickly become an idol, as we begin to believe that life is merely a construct of our DNA, and that genetic modification is no different than tweaking the operation of a machine.

But that is not to say we should shut it down. My mother has Alzheimer's. I don't want to impede anybody's progress in finding a cure or a means of prevention. Genetic technology can dramatically speed up the creation of flu vaccines, a critical ability for our overall health. Genetic science offers some incredible hope, and I believe that God calls and inspires geneticists just as surely as preachers and teachers. God also calls corporations to earn enough to provide capital for such efforts. But profit cannot be the only voice at the table. We need to walk together on this, the person of faith, the person of science, and the corporate executive, each providing checks and balances for the possible idolatry of the other.

No Engraving

The commandment about idols is very specifically a commandment about engraving—carving something into a final form that cannot be altered. This is a comfortable thing for us to do. When a thing stays the same, the rest of life is easier. We know its bounds and can structure other things around it without putting those other things in jeopardy. We like to know that things are how we left them, and we prefer to be the ones to authorize any change.

But change is a sign of life, and we Christians say we worship a living God. If we can't add some Section 8 housing units to our development plans because it will decrease our profit, if we can't challenge an interpretation of Scripture or the policies of government, if we can't even consider limiting scientific application to be sure our world is both just and safe, we are in the world of idolatry. We have taken our corporate, political, or religious ideals and carved them into stone.

Images in our churches—the icons, the banners, the video, the paintings, the sculpture—enhance our worship. It is not until we find ourselves saying that worship is impossible without a video projector or until we condemn the representation of a black Jesus or until we defile a house of worship simply because of the presence of a statue of Mary that we have crossed the line to a graven image. When either the presence of an image or its obliteration becomes more important than loving our neighbors, the second commandment is in tatters.

3

Taking God's Name in Vain

Thou shalt not take the name of the Lord thy God in vain; for the Lord will not hold him guiltless that taketh his name in vain.

A colleague of mine was completely dismayed when he moved to a new church and heard his young son say, in the presence of members of the new congregation, "Jesus, it's hot!" The boy wasn't praying and was too young to have manufactured the phrase himself. My friend, embarrassed, looked at the members of his congregation and quickly said, "His mother taught him that."

While the Sabbath commandment may get the award for the most widely disregarded in American culture, the command not to take God's name in vain takes the prize for the most trivialized. This commandment has been watered down simply to mean not swearing when you hit your finger with a hammer and not using God's name outside of a religious context.

That interpretation has merit. Names are an important part of our identity, and other cultures have understood far better than ours how much power they contain. The Internet, ironically, is helping us rediscover this ancient truth. When we choose screen names for ourselves we're careful about who knows our real name—sharing that makes us vulnerable.

So God's name isn't to be thrown around lightly or used simply for our own gain or advantage. We shouldn't be saying, "Jesus!" if it's not a direct address, but this is one of the smaller concerns related to this commandment. The real damage comes, I believe, not from using God's name inappropriately in our speech, but by taking God's name as our own and then acting in ways opposed to God's love.

Christian doctrine says that Jesus is God in the flesh—fully human and fully God at the same time. So taking the name of Jesus Christ for ourselves—calling ourselves "Christian"—is taking God's name. The massive issue behind this commandment is whether we've taken the name of "Christian" in vain. To call ourselves "God's people" is to imply that we're acting as God's agents in the world. Acting in ways opposed to God's kingdom, then, becomes taking God's name in vain. It is vain, or futile, to take God's name and then act in ways that God would not.

As Christians, we've associated ourselves with a very particular revelation of God's will and expectations. For us, the life and teachings of Jesus reveal the way God wants us to live our lives. Jews and others may view this commandment differently. But for those who believe the words of Jesus that "The Father and I are one" (John 10:30), to take the name of Christ is to take the name of God.

Just because Timothy McVeigh claimed the name of Christ doesn't mean that blowing up the federal building in Oklahoma City was something Jesus would do. He took that name thinking he could represent Christ in his actions. He took that name in vain. There are those who would like us to believe that because they profess faith in Jesus that their actions are always those that Jesus would approve. That's not true. Whenever the actions of a Christian don't match the actions of Christ, we've taken God's name in vain.

In a speech at Yale Divinity School in March 2004, former Secretary of State Madeleine Albright told this story:

> Not long after September 11th, I was on a panel with Elie Wiesel. He asked us to name the unhappiest character in the Bible. Some said Job, because of the trials he endured. Some said Moses, because he was denied entry into the Promised Land. Some said Mary, because she witnessed the crucifixion of her son. Wiesel said he believed the right answer was God, because of the pain he must surely feel in seeing us fight, kill, and abuse each other in the Lord's name.[1]

The Hebrew word for "vain" in the Ten Commandments is *shav*, which means emptiness, lying, and falsehood. The ninth commandment tells us not to bear false witness against our neighbor. This commandment is related, for it tells us not to bear false witness against God.

Don't take Christ's name and then act like the antichrist. To do so is lying about the nature of God, and it accomplishes exactly the opposite of the Great Commission to go into the world and preach the gospel. Taking Christ's name in vain is anti-gospel and the Church has become so adept at it that people stay away in droves.

Of course unless we have achieved perfection, we all do this a lot. I don't mean to say that anyone who sins can't call themselves Christian. There wouldn't be many of us around. But we should be at the ready to confess our sins and let the world know that our actions are less than God desires from us and that God stands ready to forgive.

Evangelism

To many, the inclusion of evangelism here may seem odd, but if taking God's name is such a serious business, then we should give no less attention to the ways in which we try to persuade others to take that name. In conservative circles evangelism is a matter of both obedience and church growth, and the means of saving the lost. In liberal circles the word is almost never uttered except with disdain. But evangelism is a moral issue that grows more critical with every car bomb that explodes around the world.

The reason that liberals run from the word evangelism is that so much Christian evangelism has been tainted by abuse and atrocity. In my fundamentalist days, I was driven to evangelize, not by some authority in the church, but by my own belief that people who didn't believe as I did would burn in hell forever. Like a mother dashing for her children as they wandered toward the cliff's edge, I was manic in my attempts to save them from destruction.

My motives were loving and pure—I wanted to save them not for my own gain but because I cared. But if you truly believe (as I did) that those who don't believe as you do will suffer eternally, then any amount of temporary suffering they might have to endure to change their minds is worth it in the end. Follow that far enough, and it becomes much better that I imprison you, torture you, or brainwash you into believing the "right" things than it is for me to let you go on your merry way down the road to perdition.

Of course such evangelizing doesn't start with mind control or torture. It starts with a friendly conversation over coffee, where I present the depth of my faith and the logic of my position. But if you don't buy it—if my pitch isn't successful, my concern for your soul will drive me further. If you resist my gentle persuasion—and encourage others to do the same—I might be forced to take drastic action. And that's not just a historical oddity like the Spanish Inquisition, the Salem Witch Trials, or the Crusades. It happens today, too—consider the fate of abortion doctors who have died at the hands of those claiming to be "pro-life."

Liberals mistrust the premise of conservative evangelism, which is largely driven by the belief that those who believe wrongly are hellbound. To liberal ears, eternal punishment for limited earthly sin isn't even fair, let alone loving. Even Old Testament justice was "eye for eye and tooth for tooth." To be punished without end for sins that had an end is not even "eye for eye," let alone "turn the other cheek."

Since liberals distrust the conservative portrayal of hell and the nature of God it implies, evangelism doesn't get a second glance, except in works of social justice. Though liberals have understood evangelism as living justly and helping the poor, that's only half the picture. In many liberal churches, faith-sharing will send people running for cover.

That represents a failure of imagination. There are other motivations for evangelism than the fear of hell. I have been amazed that even purely secular concerns, like more people in the pews or more money in the plate, have not been motivation enough, as many churches struggle for survival. Leaving self-interest aside, however, evangelism and the fulfillment of Jesus' command to go and make disciples are not practices that have to be based in fear. Look at the Samaritan woman at the well in John 4 who becomes a successful evangelist for her entire town. Why? She's so amazed at Jesus that she can't help but tell everyone about him.

Nowhere in that story is anybody threatened or coerced. How does the woman get her neighbors interested? Does she threaten they'll be left behind if they don't believe her? No. Verse 39 says, "Many Samaritans from that city believed in him because of the woman's testimony, 'He told me everything I have ever done.'"

As the Samaritan woman at the well shows, evangelism is all about sharing our excitement about a relationship we've found and telling about our own faith experiences. For Christians, the excitement isn't about a set of doctrines but about a person—God in human flesh, and about the way that knowledge revolutionizes how we live together on this planet. We've discovered that God has consented to be known—not completely known, but known enough to form a relationship that helps us recognize him in the face of other human beings. That's good news too incredible not to be shared. Real Christian evangelism isn't coercion; it's sharing our joy in our relationship with Jesus. This does not need to be offensive.

When I first discovered the books in the seventh grade, I was a one-person *Lord of the Rings* lending library and an evangelist for the books. If I met you and you hadn't read them, I'd share my love of them with such passion that you'd sign up to be next on the list to read my copies, which circulated through my classes. I did it all over again when Peter Jackson's movies started coming out. It didn't matter that you told me you didn't like fantasy. I still sang my song of praise in the hopes that you'd go see it anyway. I'd pay your way if you went with me, not because I thought you'd lose your family and home if you didn't, but because my life had been so totally enriched by the experience that I wanted to give you that chance, too.

Nobody gets offended when someone shares their excitement about a book or a movie or a restaurant. We even put up with good friends dragging us to places we never otherwise would have gone and at least recognize that having some understanding of what others love helps our relationship to grow, even if we don't love the thing ourselves.

So if I don't tell you about my faith, it's either because it doesn't interest me or because I don't care about you (or am afraid of you). I'd love to hear Muslims tell me what they find life-enriching and fulfilling in Islam, so that my own understanding of God and of them can grow. And I'd want to share with them how the concept of incarnation allows me to see God even in "the least of these."

Biblical evangelism is not coercive or manipulative. It's an act of sharing incredible news, and an invitation to a meeting. Anyone is free to decline the invitation or to disbelieve the witness. If our presentation is passionless, no one will be interested. If the God we are introducing will send us to hell if we don't believe, people will be either repulsed or enslaved.

I think the woman at the well had it just right. Go and tell people about the amazing encounter you've had. Pique their curiosity so they'll go and see for themselves. Then get out of the way and let Jesus take over. Our job is to make the introduction, not to manage the relationship.

If we could understand that, maybe we could have our faith and world peace, too; we might have interfaith dialogue rather than our current condition of interfaith massacres or segregation. Religions of all sorts have run amok, each with its own fundamentalist fringe ready to blow up those who disagree. This is a moral issue for all Christians because in hardcore evangelism the name of Jesus is being associated with atrocity and violence. People are taking Christ's name in vain. Evangelism like that of the Samaritan woman breaks down rather than inflames ethnic rivalries and hatreds, sharing out of loving respect rather than self-righteous condemnation. It invites rather than pushes.

Christians have a moral obligation to share the news of incarnation with the world. God has consented to live in human flesh, and whatever is done to the least of our brothers and sisters—to the prisoner at Abu Ghraib, to the woman in the Congo, to the illegal immigrant crossing our border—is done to God. Things would be so different if we could realize that.

If we'd stop taking the name of Christ in vain, we might help solve— rather than exacerbate—the divisiveness of our world.

Baptism

Christians first take God's name in baptism. Most denominations agree that at the moment of baptism a person becomes part of the Body of Christ. At our baptism we take not only the name of Christ as our own, but his mission as well, as we become part of the continuing incarnation of Jesus in the world.

That's why Christians need to be especially vigilant against unthinkingly baptizing political platforms, social agendas, and moral issues as "Christian." Human beings are the only proper subjects for baptism. Only people can take Christ's name.

Any American who has ever watched the news is familiar with the phrase "Christian Right." In response there are some who are beginning to talk about the "Christian Left." That's dangerous terminology. The ideologies of the right or left wings of the political spectrum are not the proper objects of baptism. Baptismal vows reflect our relationship to Jesus Christ, not to a political or social stance.

While people who use the term "Christian Right" mean those people on the political right who are Christians, the constant use of the phrase has convinced many that those who hold conservative values are all Christian and that those who are Christian all hold conservative values. Many Democrats like me are tired of people assuming we're Republicans when we profess our faith. When I tell someone my profession, I've always had some explaining to do because of my gender. Now I have to add more disclaimers because so many people are unable to hear the word "Christian" without "Right" being attached to it.

At a book signing for my first book, *Blowing the Lid Off the God-Box*, an elderly woman showed up, loaded down with news clippings of the Democratic take on national and world events. She'd seen that a minister would be signing books and assumed that I was part of the "Christian Right." She didn't even come for the discussion, but showed up at the end to have some private time to try to sway me to her views. She was quite surprised to learn she was preaching to the choir.

Good Christians can be found on all sides of the complex moral issues we face. There is no one "Christian" side, and to imply that there is breaks the third commandment—it's falsely taking the name of Christ and pinning it on an improper object. Baptism is for people, not for social agendas. It would be better to baptize the cat.

Christians should take stands on the issues that face us. If our faith is real, it becomes the lens through which we look at all of life, and to carve out certain parts of life as beyond God's concern is to misunderstand what Christian faith is all about. While the "Christian Right" has equated their agenda with Christian faith, Christians on the left—or even in the center—have not seemed to be able to gather the momentum to protest those assumptions and to reclaim their baptism.

It does matter. Those outside the church watch the baptized to understand what Christian faith is about, but baptizing political platforms and social ideologies as "Christian" presents a false image of Christ. Genesis tells us that human beings—not nations or special-interest groups—are made in the image of God. "Christian" defines a person who is in a particular relationship to Jesus Christ. It is not an adjective.

Christian Nation

When Constantine declared that the Roman Empire would adopt Christianity as the state religion, Christians were undoubtedly relieved. Previously, they'd endured persecutions that can hardly be talked about without at least an R rating for violence. They were forbidden many of the freedoms granted to others, and harassed and abused wherever they went. Having the emperor throw such enormous support their way must have been a huge relief.

Some wonderful things happened as a result of that sudden truce. With secret meetings a thing of the past, early Christians could give artistic expression to their joyful faith. They created houses of worship that rivaled pagan temples in their beauty and splendor, paintings and sculptures that told the Christian story, music that expressed their faith, and drama that re-enacted the Gospel for all who would listen. Schools for training priests sprang up. By the Middle Ages theology was known as "The Queen of the Sciences." The support of the Holy Roman Empire made all this possible.

But there was a dark side. Constantine didn't just free Christians to worship without persecution. He married the state and the Church. To hold a religious office as a priest or bishop was also to hold a position of political power and influence. The rule of the Church was the rule of the state, with all the money and prestige and even armies that had always come with the latter.

During the days of the New Testament, the task for every Christian was finding a way to remain faithful to Jesus. As those early Christians began to structure themselves and choose leadership, the task was re-defined. Then the job of the Church as a corporate body was to figure out how to be faithful to Jesus, and the job of the Christian was to be faithful to the institutional Church. Once Constantine joined Church and empire the business of being a Christian changed again. Now it was the job of the state to be faithful to Jesus, the Church to be faithful to the state, and the Christian to be faithful to the Church.

In a sinless society, that's not a problem. In fact, the Kingdom of Israel had a similar arrangement in the years of the early kings, and if it hadn't been for the Roman occupation, Israel would have been operating under much the same structure in Jesus' day. Of course God had tried to warn Israel back in the days of Samuel that such a structure would bring trouble, because society is *not* sinless. But God honored the freedom to choose their own form of government and anointed their kings, and I'm willing to give Constantine's famous dream the benefit of considerable doubt and say that he began with God's anointing.

Positions of unchecked power and money are dangerous to a Christian's soul. Jesus himself refused such a position as he refused to be a political and military savior and took the way of the cross instead. During the same Yale Divinity School speech quoted earlier, Madeleine Albright also said this:

> Nations are neither baptized nor promised salvation. But if they were, is it fair to ask whether a rich nation would be comparable to a rich

man, no more likely to reach heaven than a camel is to walk through the eye of a needle? We are a generous people. And I have said many, many times that I am proud to be an American. But our country does rank dead last among industrialized nations in the proportion of our wealth that we share with the developing world. [Opposing terrorism] is not the end; it is the beginning. Because terrorism is not the world's only evil. And extremists are not the only ones prone to confuse what is profoundly wrong with something else.[2]

The dilemma of the rich man who's unable to go through the eye of the needle (and perhaps also the story of the Rich Young Ruler who could not give up his possessions) is exactly the difficulty that the Holy Roman Empire began to face. Wealth means power, and those in power don't give it up readily—as a quick glance through history (or the morning paper) will tell you. Let's say a young priest has suddenly had his eyes opened to a new way of understanding Scripture. He begins to teach it and gain a following for his opinion. His leadership skills are honed in the process and it begins to look like he could climb the ranks in the church and become a bishop or even an archbishop.

But having a new bishop means the old bishop loses his appointment. And losing his appointment means losing his wealth, which means losing his status, influence, and power. If he hasn't been corrupted by his wealth and power and sees the light of God in the young priest's eyes, he may graciously step aside and make room for his successor. But this doesn't happen often. More frequently the old bishop ferociously holds onto his power, condemning the young priest's ideas as heresy to prevent his rise. The young priest is faced with a choice: recanting his position and keeping his parish or being tossed out. And if the young priest presents a really big threat, he can be burned at the stake.

Some historians claim that every pronouncement of heresy (and thus the formation of orthodoxy) was the result of such political power-wrangling. Others claim that the Church has always remained above corruption. I doubt both of those positions, although during some periods of history, depending on the character of the pope at the time, the truth might have been much closer to one extreme or the other.

I wonder if Martin Luther would have needed to break with the Church and start the Protestant Reformation if Church and state had never been joined. The abuses in the Church in the 1500s might not have developed if the Church hierarchy hadn't had such access to wealth and power. Christians needed to be freed from persecution but the creation of the Holy Roman Empire, making the Church and the state one, was one of the most dangerous actions of all time.

If the Holy Roman Empire hadn't happened, Constantine might have tried to crush the Arabs anyway. But if those state wars hadn't been associated with the Church—if the fight had been the Roman Empire against the Ottoman Empire rather than Christians against Infidels—would Muslim extremists have flown planes into the World Trade Center? Maybe. But maybe not. Keeping Church and state separate might have helped future governments do the same, perhaps providing a model for how religion could be engaged within the political sphere without being co-opted by it. Jesus refused to command armies though he easily could have done so. If Jesus didn't see war as his mission, and Christians are the Body of Christ, shouldn't our mission be the same as his?

Power and money corrupt. It's not rocket science. Christians who helped form the United States government and write the Constitution were well aware of that, so they ensured freedom of religious expression but refused to directly tie the nation to any one religion. They included a system of checks and balances to prevent one party from gaining too much power and influence. However pure a "Christian nation" might be at its outset, I believe its end is tyranny. A nation cannot be baptized as Christian—that's a fast track to idolatry, which puts God's name on something that is not God. It is taking God's name in vain.

Taking God's name upon ourselves—adopting the name "Christian" —shouldn't be done lightly. It should be proclaimed boldly, and solemnly, in a public setting. Taking God's name means binding ourselves to God's covenant, accepting both its rewards and its discipline. Only a human being can make that choice and be a part of that covenant. That's one of the reasons we sing, "The church is not a building, the church is not a steeple, the church is not a resting place. The church is a people." When we talk about "The Christian Church," we are talking about the people.

When our baptism honors us with the name Christian, the world watches us to see what the name of Christ stands for. We must not take that name in vain.

Remember the Sabbath

Remember the Sabbath day, to keep it holy. Six days shalt thou labour, and do all thy work: But the seventh day is the Sabbath of the Lord thy God: in it thou shalt not do any work, thou, nor thy son, nor thy daughter, thy manservant, nor thy maidservant, nor thy cattle, nor thy stranger that is within thy gates: For in six days the Lord made heaven and earth, the sea, and all that in them is, and rested the seventh day: wherefore the Lord blessed the Sabbath day, and hallowed it.

I went away to a cabin in the woods to work on this book. I left Sunday after church. Monday morning, as Hurricane Katrina was wiping the Gulf coast off the map, the church secretary called me on my cell phone to say she was quitting. The days reserved for quiet writing and reflection were suddenly filled with phone calls, e-mails, and decision-making—trying to figure out (long-distance) how to handle the situation in the church office, trying to coordinate a disaster response for the church.

A quiet moment came, and I grabbed my laptop, all the more anxious about the manuscript deadline that drew ever closer. I put the title on this chapter and suddenly said, "Hey, wait a minute—what's wrong with this picture?" It was Thursday, the first sunny day of a stressful week. I closed my laptop and went out for a Sabbath walk.

The commandment to keep the Sabbath is the most widely ignored of all the commandments. At least in American culture, we seem to be bent on wiping it right off the stone tablets. Every year people appear more harried, more tired, and less satisfied with their labors. Every year another store or corporation decides to extend hours around the clock and across the week. Those that don't may have given many of their employees so much to do that they take work home and labor round the clock anyway.

When a war is declared or a prisoner executed, people talk about the commandment not to kill. The adultery commandment is broken a lot, but there still seems to be a general acknowledgment that God has forbidden it. We fuss about idols, even though we may disagree on what they are, and we wrestle with how to honor fathers and mothers who don't seem to us to be worthy of such respect.

But though people are falling asleep at the wheel from a lack of rest and are coming back tired from their vacations to workloads so impossible it would have been better not to have left, despite long hours and overwork and constant demands on everyone's time, I never hear Christians say, "Hey, there's a commandment about that. God commanded that we rest—regularly—one day out of every seven." (Just a little biblical perspective here, resulting from a quick check on my concordance software: The word Sabbath(s) is mentioned 172 times in the King James Version. Even words related to idolatry get only 131. Adultery has 69 mentions, murder 43, stealing 28, and coveting a paltry 23.)

The Sabbath commandment is one of the longest of the ten, and its foundation differs, depending on whether you read the version in Exodus or Deuteronomy. In Exodus, we're to rest because rest is part of the very structure of creation. God worked for six days and rested on the seventh. God could have worked for six days, said, "There, it's done!" and gone on to the next project. Instead, God worked rest into the very fabric of the created order. There are seven days in a week, not six, because one is devoted to rest.

In Deuteronomy, the command to rest is founded in justice. The people of Israel are to remember what it was like when they were slaves in Egypt and had no rest. They are to rest one day out of every seven to avoid repeating those conditions, both for themselves and for anyone—human or animal, slave or free—within their society. They are to remember what oppression felt like and put this provision into their legal system so that such oppression could not happen again, to anybody.

Both aspects apply to this commandment, and both are foundational to living as a healthy community. But the Christian community only seems to complain about Sabbath breaking when sports teams have games on Sunday mornings.

One of the other places Sabbath is mentioned is in Exodus 31:12–17.

> The Lord said to Moses: You yourself are to speak to the Israelites: "You shall keep my sabbaths, for this is a sign between me and you throughout your generations, given in order that you may know that I, the Lord, sanctify you. You shall keep the sabbath, because it is holy for you; everyone who profanes it shall be put to death; whoever does any work on it shall be cut off from among the people. Six days shall work be done, but the seventh day is a sabbath of solemn rest, holy to the Lord; whoever does any work on the sabbath day shall be put to death. Therefore the Israelites shall keep the sabbath, observing the sabbath throughout their generations, as a perpetual covenant. It is a sign for ever between me and the people of Israel that in six days the Lord made heaven and earth, and on the seventh day he rested, and was refreshed."

Pretty strong language. Not only is breaking the Sabbath law a capital offense, but keeping it is a sign of God's eternal covenant with God's people. While other parts of the Ten Commandments have parallels in other legal materials in the ancient Near East and elsewhere, the commandment to rest (along with the prohibition against idols) is unique to Jewish law.[1] It sets the people of God apart from surrounding nations and speaks to the unique nature of Israel's God.

The loss of Sabbath is a much greater contributor to the destruction of family and societal life than the divorce rate, homosexuality, video games, or any of the other things that people like to blame for our current state of affairs. The Bible makes a big, huge, hairy deal out of keeping the Sabbath, while Christians who jump up and down to hang the Ten Commandments on every street corner act as if it's not even there, or as if it's obsolete and far less important than other issues that the Bible mentions only in passing.

Sabbath-keeping affects us each as individuals, but there are also ways that the Sabbath impacts how we act as a society—and as a global community.

Capitalism

Cast your eyes down the list of the people who aren't supposed to work on the Sabbath and it's plain that justice is an important part of the Sabbath day. It isn't just the business owner who gets a break. Every worker, every slave, every foreigner—even every working animal—is to have a full day off from labor.

But these days, it's only the wealthy who can take time off. There are millions who must work more than one job just to put food on the table. At one point my brother was holding down three jobs. He was lucky to get four hours of sleep a night, let alone a day off. Too many people today work with no paid vacation time and can't afford a vacation because they can't afford not to have a paycheck.

These are people who are faced with unjust choices. No one should have to choose between food or shelter and rest. We need them all, and God's law tries to ensure that rest is provided for all. But we ignore this law. Call me cynical or anti-business, but from out here in the trenches, this free-market society seems perfectly willing to sacrifice human beings on the altar of profit. The ads say that the stores stay open all night "for our convenience," but I'm not aware of stores which stay open twenty-four hours if doing so cuts into profits, no matter how "convenient" others find it.

And if the store is open, someone must work—someone who probably wasn't involved in the decision to stay open for twenty-four hours, but who can't afford to quit, even though she now has no one to care for the baby overnight.

Certainly larger forces can end up affecting the bottom line of both small and large corporations. We saw that in the wake of 9/11 and Hurricane Katrina. But the economic pain isn't shared fairly. CEOs don't sacrifice a dime in salary or benefits when a company goes bankrupt, but the lowly worker gets the pink slip, loses medical insurance, or takes a cut in pay. Those "lucky" few who keep their employment are now required to do more with less—the very slave conditions that Deuteronomy warns the people never to forget.

But our system is even more insidious. Wayne Muller, in *Sabbath: Finding Rest, Renewal, and Delight in Our Busy Lives,* points out that the worldwide standard for measuring the health of a country is an economic standard. It's the Gross Domestic Product or GDP. When lots of money changes hands, the GDP goes up, we say the economy is booming, and we believe we're well. When there's little exchange, the GDP goes down, and we get worried.

What that means, in a practical sense, is that if we suddenly stopped buying all that stuff we don't need and accepted a lower standard of living so we could work fewer hours and have more time to read to our children, take a walk in the woods, or care for a sick neighbor, the GDP would plunge and the media would proclaim that we were in an economic decline—which would send us into a panic that our nation was falling apart. But if we start a war, we can put a lot of people to work and exchange huge amounts of money. People will die and be left homeless and maimed for life—but our GDP will soar as we spend millions to deal with the fallout, and we'll proclaim ourselves to be in good shape.

Muller goes on to say:

> Every time someone gets cancer, the GDP goes up. Every time an infant dies, the GDP rises. A drive-by shooting improves the economy by $20,750. If the victim dies, and there is a murder trial, the benefit to the economy leaps to well over $100,000. An oil tanker spill can contribute between five and twenty million dollars of "growth"; the benefits of an airline crash or terrorist bombing can be far greater . . . In short, we have converted destruction into an economic good. But anything that grows without money changing hands—parents who care for their children, people who voluntarily care for the sick, the dying, or the homeless, people who pray or meditate or walk in the woods—these at best have no value. At worst, they take away precious time and energy that could be used to grow the GDP.[2]

Can capitalism and Sabbath co-exist? I don't have the expertise to answer that question, but I think it's a question that Christians should ask.

Jubilee

While we ponder economics, the fourth commandment leads us to the way the Law of Moses interpreted what it meant to remember the Sabbath and keep it holy. That interpretation is some of the most radical economic thinking in the Bible, far outstripping the early experiments in communal living by the first disciples. Check out Leviticus 25, which commands that every seven weeks of years (that is, every forty-nine years), Israel must stop the economy, wipe every slate clean, and celebrate for year number fifty.

Everything stops in the Jubilee year—borrowing and lending practices, buying and selling. Houses revert back to their original owners, slaves are set free, and making a profit from food or taking interest in advance is prohibited.

We could wish the chapter went a bit further—Israelite slaves, for instance, are the only ones set free. (How quickly Israel has forgotten their own slavery as they are allowed to keep slaves from other nations and presumably profit from non-Israelites!) But the command—however limited—to free the slaves is unprecedented—though we have no evidence it was actually ever followed. Commandments that deeply affect the pocketbook rarely are.

But what did come from this grand Sabbath of Sabbaths is the Jubilee as a contemporary movement to forgive the debt of impoverished nations. The Jubilee has been celebrated by the Roman Catholic Church for millennia and the practice of opening a Holy Door began with Pope Martin V in 1423 at the Basilica of Saint John Lateran. At that time the Jubilee was celebrated every thirty-three years; now it's every twenty-five.

The Roman Catholic Church has always seen the Jubilee as an opportunity to forgive debt, but until the Jubilee of 2000 that was interpreted strictly as the spiritual debts incurred by sin. The year of Jubilee signaled pardon for those suffering in purgatory. Because of the relationship to the concept of purgatory and the association with indulgences, Protestant churches have been very reluctant to join in the ceremonies over past years.

But Jubilee 2000 was a different story. People began to talk about forgiving some of the more tangible debts of the world and freeing people not from spiritual purgatory, but from physical hell. Here are a few of the facts, as recorded on Jubileeusa.org, that fueled some of the debate:

- Nigeria borrowed $5 billion, has paid $16 billion to date, and still owes $32 billion.
- Experts estimate it would take an annual commitment of $10–15 billion to turn around the AIDS crisis in Africa that claims 7,000 lives a day.
- Sub-Saharan Africa pays almost $15 billion in debt service to the wealthy nations and institutions every year. Do the math.
- After debt relief and the elimination of school fees, 1.5 million children returned to school in Tanzania almost overnight.

Noam Chomsky wrote in *Z Magazine* about Jubilee 2000. While he advised proceeding with caution, he noted the following:

When the U.S. took over Cuba 100 years ago it cancelled Cuba's debt to Spain on the grounds that the burden was "imposed upon the people of Cuba without their consent and by force of arms." Such debts were later called "odious debt" by legal scholarship, "not an obligation for the nation" but the "debt of the power that has incurred it," while the creditors who "have committed a hostile act with regard to the people" can expect no payment from the victims. Rejecting a British challenge to Costa Rican laws cancelling the debt of the former dictator to the Royal Bank of Canada, the arbitrator—U.S. Supreme Court Chief Justice William Howard Taft—concluded that the Bank lent the money for no "legitimate use," so its claim for payment "must fail." The logic extends readily to much of today's debt: "odious debt" with no legal or moral standing, imposed upon people without their consent, often serving to repress them and enrich their masters.[3]

It's been about 3,500 years since someone first penned (or chiseled) God's command for a great Sabbath of Sabbaths to set the people free from debt, a Jubilee heralded by the ram's horn trumpet blown at the year's announcement. But in all those years, it's never really been tried. We are all too afraid of losing, too afraid of economic collapse for ourselves while other nations cannot even care for their own people. The Jubilee year is something Christians who want to take Sabbath seriously should be talking about.

Bankruptcy

What about the personal debt crushing our own citizens? Yes, we do get ourselves into a lot of the mess we're in—we buy things we don't need or don't even truly want. We have shopping addictions, we're spoiled and think we should be able to have it all—and too often we go into debt to get it.

I know about those things. The first consumer credit cards came out in my lifetime. I think our family was the first one in town to have a new Master Charge, as it was called then. I was a young teen and didn't really understand that the toys, sound equipment, and gadgets that started appearing in our home weren't really paid for. I didn't understand about interest, let alone compound interest. But I can tell you that if it wasn't for a lot of life insurance and my father's untimely death at age forty-seven, my family would have been filing for bankruptcy. Now, twelve years after my graduation from seminary, I have finally paid off my student loans. I am still paying on the credit card debt that paid my other expenses in that time. I know about those things.

I also know that there are loan sharks, and that those who can least afford to pay are charged the highest interest rates. They are slapped with ungodly fees, the rates soar, and there is no opportunity in a lifetime to pay off the debt. Some states have no caps on interest charges. Like Nigeria, people pay thousands upon thousands more than what was originally borrowed and are still no closer to paying off their debt than they ever were. It is a form of slavery.

Those suffering with personal debt in America have the option of bankruptcy, a bottom cap that poor nations do not have, but there were those who abused the system and so the laws were tightened. Note that they were only tightened for *individuals* who abused the system—not for the large corporations who account for the largest dollar amounts lost and not for the credit card companies with unjust lending practices.

The new personal bankruptcy law passed in 2005 does nothing to rein in the solicitation of credit cards. It doesn't put caps on interest rates or late fees, or make exceptions for those with catastrophic medical expenses.

The Peninsula Peace and Justice Center in Palo Alto, California, reported recently that since 1999, credit card companies have given $25 million to federal candidates and political parties, and commercial banks have given $76.2 million. They also cite a recent Harvard study indicating that about half of all personal bankruptcies are due to illness and medical bills.[4]

Maybe the law was needed. Maybe it was the right thing to do. Maybe the fact that divorced women are 300 percent more likely than single or married women to find themselves in bankruptcy court, and that African-American and Latino homeowners are 500 percent more likely than white homeowners to file for bankruptcy, doesn't point to any racial or class bias. Maybe it's just coincidence.

But whether you believe the laws are unjust or that people are irresponsible, the societal consequences of soaring debt affect us all. If all my money is going to repay debt, I can't contribute to the economy by buying from your business. I can't give more to support the ministries of the church or other non-profit groups. With their ministries limited, either the government picks up the tab, which increases taxes, or the people fall through the cracks, which increases social unrest and its associated ills. Most Christians weekly or even daily ask God to "forgive us our debts, as we forgive our debtors." We ought to be talking seriously about doing just that.

The Land

The Law of Moses further expanded the Sabbath commandment in Leviticus 25 by regulating agriculture. The fourth commandment in Deuteronomy and Exodus mentions giving people and animals a break; Levitical laws expand that to the land.

A Sabbatical year came every seventh year; it was a time when nobody could plant seed or work to grow anything but eat only what's naturally produced by the land. (Good luck if you have terminator seeds!) Like the gift of manna in the wilderness, God promises that the harvest in year six will be especially plentiful, giving people enough stored food to live while the tilled earth takes a much-needed vacation.

This is good for the earth and good for future crops. It replenishes the soil. It is also an impossible practice for the farmer in debt. No crop means no income means the banker comes and takes the farm. Israel apparently didn't respond well to giving up a year's harvest either. We know that because in 2 Chronicles 36:21 the chronicler claims that part of the reason God allowed the horror of the Babylonian exile was "to fulfill the word of the Lord by the mouth of Jeremiah, until the land had made up for its Sabbaths. All the days that it lay desolate it kept Sabbath, to fulfill seventy years." I'm not sure I buy the chronicler's theology, but clearly Israel wasn't good about keeping the Sabbath of the land, and only a few people remembered that this was a violation of God's law. This is probably one of the reasons why we find Creation "groaning" in Romans 8:22.

Lots of things to do with the Sabbath of the land go beyond the simple facts of crop rotation. Housing development run amok, for example, is slowly creating an ecological and economic crisis. Consider these statements from a fact sheet put out by the American Farmland Trust.

- Productive agricultural land is a finite and irreplaceable natural resource.
- According to USDA's National Resources Inventory (NRI), from 1992 to 1997 more than 11 million acres of rural land were converted to developed use—and more than half of that conversion was agricultural land.
- Over the past 20 years, the acreage per person for new housing almost doubled.
- The U.S. food and farming system contributes nearly $1 trillion to the national economy—or more than 13 percent of the gross domestic product—and employs 17 percent of the labor force.

Anybody can do the math. God took a lot of time to craft laws about the proper care of the land. Why don't we heed them? To suggest that the prohibitions against homosexuality in Leviticus 18:22 and 20:13 might reflect a cultural bias rather than eternal truth is tantamount to heresy in many circles. How come those same biblical defenders aren't as interested in the issue that was the focus of a whole chapter? Who will remind us of God's Sabbath for the land?

Consider this information from the Wilderness Society:

- 44.2 million acres (over 11 percent) of private forests, particularly in the East where most private forests occur, are likely to see dramatic increases in housing development in the next three decades.
- By 2050, Forest Service researchers estimate that an additional 23 million acres of forest lands in net may be lost.[5]

Maybe you're not a forest-lover. But consider this information from the same source.

- Forests supply over 50 percent of fresh water flow in the lower 48 states.
- According to Forest Service estimates, some 180 million people depend upon forests for their drinking water.
- Private forests in the southern United States alone produce more timber than both public and private forests of any other country.[6]

Christians serious about keeping God's commandments need to be serious about preserving our environment. God is quite clear in Leviticus 25:23, "The land shall not be sold in perpetuity, for the land is mine; with me you are but aliens and tenants." Aliens and tenants. We do not own the earth. We are stewards of God's earth, and the owner has told us that we are to give the land a break. We are to protect it and not exploit it for profit. We can enjoy its bounty, but we may not use it up.

As I write this, New Orleans is both under water and out of control in the wake of Hurricane Katrina. The Coalition to Restore Coastal Louisiana has been shouting for far too long that erosion of the delta marsh on the Louisiana coast was gradually making New Orleans a sitting duck, but no one would provide the funds either for the land or for the levees. In the wake of Hurricane Katrina, the land—and the people—are still groaning.

Humane Farming

The commandments in Exodus and Deuteronomy order rest for the animals, too. Since we don't give any rest to human life, it's no surprise that animal life isn't considered except for the profit it might bring. God, however, is clear in Scripture that we don't own the creatures. Look at Psalm 50:10: "For every wild animal of the forest is mine, the cattle on a thousand hills." Animal farmers take note. Those animals are not yours, no matter how much you paid for them. They are God's cows, God's pigs, God's chickens, God's sheep, and you have been charged with their care.

Every time the issue of humane farming is raised, someone pipes up to say that the abuse of farm animals is a myth and that animals on factory farms are treated just fine. Well, maybe some are. But the Humane Farming Association has successfully prosecuted and shut down some farms that were decidedly not "okay." Court decisions have shown that abuse is happening. What's the truth? Go visit a large industrial animal farm and see for yourself.

In the interest of self-disclosure, my tree-hugging tendencies are nothing compared to my zeal to treat wildlife well. I've been known to wage campaigns to save woodchucks, rodents of all sorts, and most anything else that lives and breathes, so the thought of what animals endure on factory farms is almost too much for me to bear.

But even those who aren't environmentalists—or those who don't take the biblical mandates to heart—should be concerned about the humane treatment of animals.

The Food Animal Concerns Trust (FACT) is an organization that promotes better methods of raising livestock and poultry. As you scratch your way down to the bottom of the abuse at industrial farms, you'll find (surprise, surprise) greed. Force-fed poultry, hormone-laced cows with udders too big for their bodies and prone to infection (hormones courtesy of Monsanto, the same company that brought you terminator seeds), and hogs in pens where they can't even turn around and never see the light of day, all have their origins in farmers looking for greater profit.

The Food Animal Concerns Trust (FACT) shows that treating farm animals humanely can still earn a healthy profit. Their Nest Eggs project is one success story as told on their website.

> In 1984 FACT launched the Nest Eggs project to demonstrate that farmers could profitably produce eggs without the cages that are usu-

ally used for housing hens. Typically five hens are crammed into each 12 by 18 inch cage; 24,000 cages are crammed into each hen house! It is a miracle that the birds not only live but continue to lay eggs in this dreadful environment.

Nest Eggs became one of the most successful humane programs ever launched. Over 950,000 hens were freed from cages on Nest Eggs farms and the Nest Eggs marketing concept has been widely copied across the country by many producers.[7]

One group, at least, seems to have found a way to give some Sabbath to hens and still turn a profit. More than that, they've managed to prove that the food was safer. I'll bet God knew that when the law was given.

FACT and other organizations are also working to help stop the spread of mad cow disease, which finds its way into the human food chain when we turn "downer cows" (those who are too sick to stand up) into hamburger. With mad cow crossing our border, the FDA woke up in 2004 and banned such diseased-cow burgers. It's hard to believe we ever thought that was a good idea, even with all concerns for humane treatment of the cow put aside. But the dollar rules and, according to FACT, the FDA is still getting pressure to reverse the ban.

Ironically, the cow whose demise provided mad-cow-infected hamburger to six states and the U.S. territory of Guam was a dairy cow that couldn't stand because of calving injuries, one of the side effects of the bovine growth hormone. Cows are vegetarians but they're often fed on ground-up cow—a far cry from the Law of Moses which forbids cooking a kid in its mother's milk (Exod 23:19).

Consider how many diseases that cause fear of a huge pandemic are related to animals kept in inhumane conditions: avian flu, swine flu, SARS, mad cow. The God who cared enough to mention the care of animals in the Ten Commandments can't be pleased with such things. When is their Sabbath?

There are also environmental concerns. Factoryfarm.org provides these facts about hog farming:

- In 1999, 105 farms having over 50,000 pigs accounted for 40 percent of the U.S. hog industry. The largest four operations accounted for nearly 20 percent of U.S. hog production.
- One hog alone can excrete up to 17.5 pounds of manure and urine each day.
- On a factory farm with 35,000 hogs, over 4 million pounds of feces and urine are produced each week.

Where's all that going to go? No wonder God told the Hebrews not to get involved with pork! The environmental damage done by large hog farms is obvious to anyone driving by. There are ways to have a profitable hog farm and not abuse the hogs or pollute the environment. But we have to want to do it. We have to assume that the one whose eye is on the sparrow also watches out for pigs.

Of course there are those who would see the very term "humane farming" as an oxymoron when the whole purpose of having the animal is to kill it and eat it. We take up vegetarianism in the chapter on the sixth commandment. And I could have easily filled this section with horror stories of the real animal abuse happening at this moment on large industrial animal farms. Get on the Internet and see pictures for yourself.

In our consumer culture we are fast consuming ourselves. Ignoring the command to rest ourselves, those who work for us, and the animals and land that provide our food is, quite literally, killing us.

We run ever faster in the hamster wheel of life, thinking that the speed of the wheel will save us. Technology that helps us do things faster has not lightened our load. We've ignored the command to rest and filled the time with more work. Even our play is now work. High school soccer teams practice or play six days a week in my town.

I doubt that a return to the blue laws is the answer. In general, they provided rest for only some and imposed undue burdens on others. But we can begin to address the problem if we recognize that it's systemic. Every time I hear talk about Sabbath in church, it is portrayed as an individual issue. "Take a day off." If we can pull back and realize that we've created a culture where that is practically impossible, we can begin to see the kinds of large-scale, societal changes that will be necessary to keep this commandment.

The trust that God has placed in us as stewards of all of creation—from our own time and resources to the amazing and beautiful resources of the earth and its non-human inhabitants—is being roundly and soundly neglected. And there's a commandment about that. Remember the Sabbath. Remember the rest. For you. For the poor. For the creatures. For the land. We can't do it alone, but together we can find a way.

5

Honor Thy Father and Mother

Honor thy father and thy mother: that thy days may be long upon the land which the Lord thy God giveth thee.

I don't know of any words in the English language that come to us more emotionally laden than "father" and "mother." There are different emotions attached to each one, and those emotions are flattened or intensified, joyous, resentful, or sad according to our own experiences.

Before I've finished reading the verse, I've sifted through my father's sudden death at age forty-seven and remembered staying up late at night, sitting with him in the living room, wanting to have conversations that never happened. I've remembered the way he loved Christmas lights and how he thought he could drive up any ice-covered hill if Christmas carols were just playing loud enough.

I've remembered the hymns my mother taught me to sing and that now—as she suffers from Alzheimer's—that's about all she remembers of anything. I remember how she cared for me, how her own mother abandoned her, and how difficult it was to leave her that first night in a nursing home. All that and I've only read five words!

That is, I think, what makes this commandment so difficult. With some of the other commandments, we're mostly battling our own sinfulness—our spirit and our ego are fighting for control. But in this commandment I think it's different. Our efforts are overcome by our emotions related to how we experienced our own parents, how we have or have not accepted an identity as parents ourselves, and how we view our own march toward aging and death.

What the Bible Says

The entire commandment reads: "Honor your father and your mother, so that your days may be long in the land that the Lord your God is giving you." When we hear the words "father" and "mother" we tend to become children. That means this commandment is often misinterpreted to be a command to children to obey their parents, but that's not quite it. There are other commandments in the Law of Moses that deal with children and their family relationships. Obedience in children was not a major issue. Those children who didn't obey their parents didn't live terribly long.

Remember the setting of the Ten Commandments. The adult Hebrews have gathered at the foot of Mt. Sinai to hear God's law and to decide whether to become God's people and accept these commandments as the laws of their new nation. Think of it as their first Hebrew Congress, with God making this commandment one of the laws of the land, given to adults for adults. The command is for adults to give honor to their aging parents.

There have always been issues with this. If there weren't, God wouldn't have had to legislate it. When we get to the first century AD, the words of Jesus show us that it's still a problem. In Mark 7:11–13, Jesus calls people on the carpet for using religious piety as an excuse for neglecting to take care of their parents. It's not just a modern problem.

Another false assumption is that "honor" means "obey." Again, with parental language our brains shift back to childhood where obedience was the expectation in our relationship with father, mother, and other authority figures. But this commandment is about adult relationships where the expectation moves from obedience to honor. What exactly does that mean?

The word for "honor" in Hebrew is *kabed*, which means "heavy." In a negative sense it refers to a burden—something that weighs on us. In a positive sense it means to be rich—to have enough gold to bring the scales to the floor. It means to be glorious and also to be hard, which shows the complexity of the commandment. Riches are both a joy and a burden, and the word *kabed* captures all of it. Jesus himself mentions that when Jews of his day avoided this commandment, the issue was also money. So let's start there.

Inheritance

As children, our parents take care of us physically, materially, emotionally, and spiritually—at least that's the ideal. Though some parents do just the opposite out of ignorance or cruelty, and though all parents mess up in one way or another, the ideal is that parents take care of their children's needs.

But this commandment says that when we've become adults and our parents are old, we need to stop demanding their care of us and reverse the process. We need to be *kabed*—rich—with them, becoming the ones who provide for them as they once provided for us.

The issue of inheritance betrays our lack of understanding of this concept. Inheritance laws go back to the Old Testament, and they've only become more complex with time. But this commandment reminds us that our parents don't owe us an inheritance. To expect that is to remain in the role of a child, waiting to receive material care from a mother or father. Once we're adults, we become the givers, not the receivers.

It's gut-wrenchingly sad when families are broken apart by inheritance issues. One child gets what another one wants; someone feels slighted; someone the family doesn't like gets something . . . the list goes on and on. Worse, there are predator children who not only don't give to their parents, but they take away what few resources a parent may have, sometimes by not providing necessary health care and sometimes by discouraging parents from spending money on travel or a home, all so they can receive a larger inheritance.

Our parents don't belong to us. There's no biblical commandment for parents to continue to provide for their children into adulthood. The real crime isn't that your sister got the house when you know Dad meant you to have it. The real crime is that you and your sister are no longer speaking to each other and the greatest commandment to love one another has been broken.

Any inheritance we receive from a relative or friend is a gift, pure and simple. No one is obligated to leave us a dime, and when it comes to our parents it's exactly the opposite. Instead of expecting them to be rich toward us, once we reach adulthood, we are to be rich—to be *kabed*—toward them.

Nursing Homes and Infirmity

Once we accept the role of caretaker for our parents, we can also get caught in the trap of thinking that to give honor to our parents means that we must do what they want and personally meet every need, no matter the cost to ourselves or other family members—an all-or-nothing mentality. But that's not what "honor" means.

If "honor" means "weight," we can learn something from our words "gravity" and "weighty." A grave or weighty matter is a serious one, not to be dismissed lightly or considered without great care. It is important and can have major consequences. This is the attitude we should have regarding our parents.

When a parent asks something of us as adults, we're not bound to obedience. We are bound to take the request seriously. One of the largest questions of this nature is whether we can take care of an ailing parent at home or whether care outside the home is necessary. I've been extremely fortunate. Throughout her life, my mother always indicated that she would be willing to go to an assisted living facility or a nursing home if that became necessary. And she meant it. I know she meant it because when the time came in November of 2004, she went without a fuss, even though anyone could see it was tragic and hard.

She could say that because she knew that her husband and my brother and I loved her. She knew we wouldn't send her to a place where she'd languish with poor care and no visits. She knew we'd "honor" her and her situation with weight and seriousness. We'd consider all the options and do what we felt was best. I visit her each week, and every time I leave, I thank God for her understanding.

Not everyone is so lucky. Not all parents are that emotionally healthy and not all children are kind. But the commandment speaks to all sides. If your mother or father needs care, anyone professing to live by the Ten Commandments may not simply dismiss the need. There is not one right answer for what should be done. Every case is unique.

But, just as there's no one right answer, there's no one wrong answer either. It's not automatically wrong to move a parent to a facility outside the home, even if the parent doesn't want to go. We're not commanded to obey, we're commanded to honor. We take the request seriously; we give it weight. We pray; we cry; we research the options; we talk among family members; and then we do what's best for all.

The nursing home is one of the most difficult of these decisions, but not the only one. For many parents the driving issue is also important. Often, elderly parents who shouldn't still be driving fight, tooth and nail, any suggestion to turn over the keys. And well they might. When the mobility afforded by driving is a requirement for full participation in society, giving up the keys means "retiring" from much of life. Giving up that independence is a very difficult thing. When we approach them with only the harm they might do and fail to acknowledge the major loss we propose, we fail to give them honor.

We might suggest they retire from their job or volunteer work because they've become more of a problem than a help to the enterprise. We might badger them about medical tests, diet changes, or using a cane, walker, or wheelchair. In more tragic circumstances we might confront their abuse and force them to acknowledge and come to grips with harm they've done to others or themselves. Some have the incredibly difficult job of turning a parent in to authorities or to a treatment center. But in all circumstances the commandment remains the same. Give honor. Give weight. Give seriousness to their issues and concerns. Give resources when you have them; search for them in other places when you don't. Pray, seek the guidance of others, and then come to a decision that takes everyone's needs into account.

It's hard and burdensome to give honor, which is implied in the Hebrew word itself. It's heavy. But it's what we're commanded to do.

The Role of Society

In the West, especially in the United States, we're steeped in the culture of the individual, seeing ourselves as one person rather than part of a group. We ask, "What's in it for me?" before we ask, "What's in it for us?" and we almost never ask, "What's in it for them?" Our ideal living arrangement is the "single-family home." We want to privatize, to customize, and generally to manipulate everything so that it's just right for us.

Other cultures, especially in Asia and Africa, are different. They first see themselves as part of a group. A given action might be harmful to a particular individual, but if it will give overall benefit to the group, then the action is considered "good." Both of these approaches to the world have their benefits and their drawbacks. But as we consider the Ten Commandments, remember that the ancient Hebrews were a culture that thought primarily in terms of the group, not the individual, and the entire Old Testament is written from that perspective.

On Mt. Sinai, God doesn't give private instruction to all the individuals who have gathered, but offers a way of life to a people. These commandments are as much about how to structure society as they are about personal piety. Ancient Israel was a theocracy, with no separation of Church and state. God was in charge of the state, and God's laws were the laws of the land. Even when they broke down and organized themselves under a king, the king was still seen as being under God's authority, unlike other cultures where the king declared himself to *be* God.

To miss the social dimension of the Bible, especially the Old Testament, is to miss almost entirely every message it contains. So if we proclaim that we need to live by the Ten Commandments, we should be concerned with matters far beyond what individuals do in their bedrooms or doctor's offices. We should look at the systems that either enable or prevent us from living out these commandments in our common life together.

The wonderful thing about the Ten Commandments is that most of them are accepted as decent ethical principles in American society. It's probably easier to build enthusiasm for legislative support for the Ten Commandments than to get them displayed in a public place. For instance, we could get support for laws that would better protect older adults from unscrupulous children, would enforce nursing home and home care standards, and would provide more public resources to help those with aging parents.

Some businesses provide on-site day care for children. What about daycare for my mother with Alzheimer's? If she were in my workplace during the day, I wouldn't have to find time after work to fit in a visit—something harder and harder to do as we erode the fourth commandment and take no time off. That would be one way that a business could support my keeping the fifth commandment without the business needing to take any stand on religion whatsoever. Suppose nursing homes provided wireless Internet access, so that I could have longer visits, enabling me to get some work done while she naps much as would happen in a home environment.

Society can support this commandment without writing it on the wall.

Health Care

I'm not an expert in the intricacies of health care systems, insurance benefits, doctors' training, or malpractice. But you don't have to be an expert to know that health care in our society only works for the rich. I have health care insurance provided by the United Methodist Church. I pay a paltry $50 per month for that benefit, much less than many others. But it still was difficult when the doctor wanted me to have an ultrasound. Even with insurance the test still cost me $600.

The doctor wanted me to have another one to follow up. I refused. My words to the doctor went something like this. "I can't afford to spend $1,200 on a possibility. If you feel pretty sure that I'm going to die in the next week or two without this test, then I will take your advice and do it. But I have to go into debt to afford the test, and I'm not willing to do that unless you're pretty darned sure I'll have major consequences if I don't have it done."

I don't know a lot about the system, but I know that even though my mother has long-term care insurance, social security benefits, and a pension from her years as a teacher, it is still not enough to cover her care. We have more benefits in our family than many others do, and it's still difficult. What about those who don't have those resources? Suppose we have given full weight and honor to our parents in considering their needs and made the difficult decision that they need a certain level of care, but we can't afford it? Suppose Dad needs treatment for a condition, either physical or emotional, but there are no resources?

Health care is a nationwide series of systems that can either help or hinder my ability to honor my father and mother. As such, the creation of systems for affordable health care for everyone should be part of the agenda for every person wanting to live by the Ten Commandments. There may be many ways to do it—perhaps socialized medicine, perhaps another plan set in the for-profit, privatized world. Or maybe there's a creative way to combine the two. My intent isn't to make suggestions for public policy, but to say that Christians have no business thinking that the issue has nothing to do with our faith. Don't get upset that the school system won't let you pray and then ignore the fact that the health care system won't let you honor your father and mother.

Ageism

In some cultures, both ancient and modern, the older you get, the more honor you receive. The wisdom of elders is respected and sought after even when their bodies decline. Not in America and much of the West. Here, age is both feared and scorned. Anti-aging products and surgeries consume more and more of our resources, and we're so obsessed with being young that it's hard to find a birthday card for someone over twenty-five that doesn't have getting older as the main joke.

But the effects of such age-phobia are no joke. Elder abuse is either a growing problem or a problem we're more aware of—probably both. If you're in a nursing home and don't have friends or relatives who frequently and unexpectedly check on you, you may not receive good care.

The first real illness of my mother's life began at age seventy. It turned out to be Alzheimer's and some mini-strokes, but it was accompanied by a good bit of weight loss. She had test after test, some surgery, and symptoms (which were probably a result of all the anxiety) that landed her in the emergency room a couple of times. Frequently I went with her to her appointments or to the hospital, and on the whole she received good care. But there was one specialist who showed me something I hadn't seen before.

He acted as if my mother wasn't really there. His attitude showed no compassion, no humanity. It was as if we'd violated his life and wasted his time by bringing him someone he considered old. The general attitude was, "She's old. Old people get sick. Then they die. That's how it is. Live with it." I'd heard about that attitude before, but this was the first time I'd seen it for myself. It is ageism.

Ageism denies people the right to attention, compassion, and assistance because they're old and therefore deemed worthless. In a culture fixated on the body, on youth, and on production, we have little use for old bodies. We're also afraid and project our own fears of becoming old and useless outward as a hatred of our elders. This isn't news. Every so often someone tests it by making themselves up to be old and going through a day or a week in an old person's disguise. Their reports are all the same. They disappear from the public eye. People look right through them, and if they insist on attention or help, they get the same sort of disdain that the specialist showed for my mother. "Don't waste my resources. You're old."

To honor our father and mother is another way of saying that we should respect the elders among us. I'm so glad for those saints who live well into their nineties and meet the challenges of age with grace and wisdom. I resent those older women who won't tell their age—they're setting me up for a fear of life that increases with each passing year. All of us get older. Why do we teach others to fear the inevitable?

I know age brings problems, but it also brings wisdom. At forty-seven, I'm flabbier and much less flexible than I was at twenty-six. But I wouldn't be twenty-six again for all the money on the planet. In that twenty years, I've worked through a lot of emotional junk. Life has left its scars, but I am the wiser for them. I wouldn't trade.

Not that we rejoice in infirmity. I remember going on a hospital visit to see a ninety-something woman who had popped her hip out. I walked into her room and over to the bed. The first words off her lips were, "The golden years, humph!" I loved that, and in that moment she taught me something. As we age, humor is more and more important.

No, it isn't all fun and games. There's pain and illness and every sort of loss you can have right up until the loss of life itself. But we can choose how we respond to that. We can be bitter or fearful or in denial, but we can also be grateful for what still remains, amused by the ironies of the body that C. S. Lewis so aptly called "brother Ass," and confident that God can use any condition we have for God's glory and for the good of God's kingdom. I have this theory that if we could choose the latter attitudes for ourselves, we'd begin to treat the elders among us with the care and respect they deserve. I think our disdain for our elders is a projected fear of our own loss of youth and vitality, and eventually our own fear of death.

But ageism isn't just a personal issue. There are systemic injustices that show our disdain for the elderly and keep us from honoring our fathers and mothers. If we've navigated the difficult step of getting someone to give up a driver's license, that helps to keep the roads safer. But it also creates a new set of problems. The person without a license in our culture is isolated. They cannot get out to buy food, to keep doctor's appointments, or to attend church or social functions. When there is no system of public transportation or private network of transportation providers (or when such services are beyond what someone can afford), the needs of our fathers and mothers are not honored.

Sometimes family members can provide transportation, but often they cannot. The longer you live, the more likely you are to outlive other members of your family—even your children. I've presided at funerals for people where even the grandchildren were pushing the limits of offering physical help. And not everyone has a family. I purchased long-term care insurance in my early forties because I have no spouse and no children and just one sibling. There likely will be no family member to care for me when I am old; and without public systems designed to help me, I will languish.

Along with issues of transportation are issues of personal mobility and accessibility. I have a dear friend who is a quadriplegic and has been wheelchair bound for some thirty years. One of the biggest ironies in his condition is that one of the places that is not built to accommodate his condition is the doctor's office. The hallways are too narrow for his chair, the turns too sharp; and there's no way to get him up on an examining table. The concerns for the aged and the consequent limitations go beyond our private attitudes and personal activities. Those wanting to follow this commandment need to push for public aid for our elders.

Who Is My Father and Mother?

Motherhood and fatherhood go well beyond biology. Jesus shows this clearly in Matthew 12:48–50 and in the corresponding passage in Mark 3 where he essentially disregards his biological mother and siblings at the door and identifies anyone who does the will of God as his family. The question of who is a mother or a father to us is rather like the question of "Who is my neighbor?" that occasions Jesus' parable of the Good Samaritan in Luke 10. Jesus' answer to the lawyer asking that question was just like his answer to the question about who family members are. The answer is "those who behave like family," just like the answer about who is my neighbor was answered with "those who behave in a neighborly fashion." It's not about a legal status, it is about caring action. Who is my mother? The one who treats me like a daughter. Who is my father? The one who is willing to call me son.

We see this borne out in all sorts of relationships, biological and otherwise. There are those with a legal status because they literally gave us birth or went through a legal adoption or guardianship process. But then there are others who have given us the love associated with father or mother even though they have no biological or legal relationship to us whatsoever.

I call Pete and Dorothy Willingham my "surrogate parents." That causes some raised eyebrows now and again, since "surrogate" is also a legal term for someone who carries the child of another. But that's not what I mean. Pete and Dorothy are a childless couple just a bit younger than my own parents who, when my life fell apart and I was twelve-hundred miles from home, cared for me as a mother and father would care for a child. No matter that I was in my thirties; they became my parents. I believe this commandment calls me to honor them in addition to my biological parents.

In the social dimension, that means working for a society that also honors the variety of ways people can be mothers and fathers for others. Often adoptive fathers and mothers are more truly parents of a child than those who provided biological life, but that's not always recognized by the courts. I've watched television accounts of children being dragged kicking and screaming away from the only parents they've ever known—parents who love and care for them more than their own lives—because biological parents want to lay claim to them again. We need to build a society where those sorts of scenes and that sort of trauma to children cannot happen.

Gay and lesbian couples often provide far more love and care for a child than the child's other parents or guardians, but some states consider it better for a child to have no parental care at all than to have two mothers or two fathers. You can't tell me that Jesus would rather a child remain in an orphanage or in a hate-filled home than live with two people who love the child and love each other. Even if you believe homosexuality is sinful, the restriction still doesn't hold water unless you remove children from every home where sinners live. You'd have to build an awful lot of orphanages.

If we are to honor our fathers and mothers, we need a society with systems that will make it possible for us to honor all those who love and care for children.

Our Faith Parents

Of course we again have the challenge of thinking in terms of the group rather than strictly individuals, which means there may well be categories of people that could be considered "parents" for us. Whenever we quote the Gettysburg address and say, "Four score and seven years ago, our fathers brought forth upon this continent a new nation," we remember just how broad the concept of parenthood can be. We honor those fathers when we take the Constitution seriously.

We also honor our faith parents—not just individuals who have led us in our personal faith, but entire faith traditions, without whom we wouldn't have the faith we do today. For Christians, we need to remember that we were birthed by the Jews. When Christians fall into anti-Semitism, as we have time and time again over the last two thousand years, we dishonor our faith parent. Honoring the Jews doesn't have to mean obedience to Jewish law. But it does mean treating the faith of the Jews with respect and giving their concerns serious consideration—weight.

When the Jews as a community tell Christians that something we're doing or saying is causing them pain, we need to listen. Speaking up about the historical persecutions of Jews in response to portrayals of Christ's passion is one example. Christians probably won't stop telling the story that is central to our faith. But we can truly listen to the concerns that are raised and see if there are ways that we can tell the story that don't lead to violence against Jews. We can hear how "the Jews killed Jesus" has been used in murderous ways against Jews across the millennia and work to stop anti-Semitism in all its forms, both blatant and subtle. After all, the faith of the Jews was the faith of Jesus, Peter, and Paul as well as Judas, Herod, and Caiaphas.

As a Protestant, I'm also a child of the Roman Catholic Church. There's been bad blood between Protestants and Catholics ever since Luther tacked his 95 Theses to the Wittenberg door in 1517. You don't have to look beyond England, Ireland, and Scotland to see the horrors of this rivalry—atrocities committed on both sides. Protestants came into being in "protest" of some very real abuses in the medieval Catholic Church. We have some very real differences about many other things to this day.

But Protestantism was a love child. We weren't seen as legitimate, but we were very much born from Martin Luther's love of both God and the truth of Catholicism that he felt was being buried in church practice and corruption. For Protestants to scorn the Roman Catholic Church and to seek her harm or dissolution is to dishonor our faith mother. In some Protestant circles Catholics are condemned to hell at worst and considered suspect at best.

I attended a meeting to discuss ways to remember soldiers fighting overseas. It was suggested that each soldier connected to our congregation have a candle lit for them. I thought this was a lovely idea, but one woman was so deeply suspicious of what she saw as a Catholic practice that she grilled me for quite some time on why I'd thought of candles for this act, as if she were about to call the bishop and report me as a closet Catholic who'd infiltrated a United Methodist pulpit.

Protestants need to honor their Roman Catholic mother. We need not do everything she says, but as with the Jews, we need to listen— really listen—and consider how we can make life better for her when it's in our power to do so. And so it goes for all groups that have had a part in shaping our faith. Maybe you belong to a church that split off from another one over some conflict. I learned of a church in seminary that had such a split over who took the last piece of fried chicken at a church dinner. It doesn't matter who wronged who, and your own church may be right in what they decided. That's not the point. The point is to honor your parents. You wouldn't exist if it weren't for that church you split from. You are a child of that church. Give her honor.

Perhaps it seems like this has broadened the concept out too far, but the Hebrew words for father and mother in the commandment had the same scope of meaning—from (very narrowly) the people who gave you birth to the very broad concept of ancestors, founders, originators, patrons, and the like.

Not that any of this is easy, especially when the relationship has been difficult and/or abusive. Whether it's the child abused by a biological or foster parent or an altar boy abused by his priest, honoring the parent, even in the sense we're talking about here, is extremely difficult. To honor a parent in such situations falls into the category of loving your enemies, and that's never a cake walk.

But even in those situations, thinking about *kabed*—the gravity of our response to their needs—still holds up. We aren't asked to like them or to approve of what was done to us, and we're not asked to continue to put ourselves in harm's way. But we are asked, I believe, not to discard their humanity, even when their own actions seem to have waived all rights to human compassion. Perhaps it's in honoring abusive parents in this way that we become the most like Jesus.

6

Life and Death

Thou shalt not kill.

My friend Veronica and I were at an impasse. I don't know how we ended up talking about social issues, but we did, and on two important matters we simply couldn't fathom the position of the other. My issue was capital punishment. I'm against it for a lot of reasons, but the big sticking point for me is that with the death penalty we're deciding it's okay to take a God-given life, and we aren't checking with God to see if that's okay. Veronica agreed that it wasn't an easy decision, but since life without parole wasn't a fail-safe option, she felt we needed to have the death penalty to protect others.

Veronica's issue was war. A complete pacifist, she wouldn't justify going to war under any circumstances. It was not okay to just march in and kill people. Life is sacred and is not to be used as a tactic to gain political objectives. I agreed that war was a terrible thing, but I was willing to allow for a time when taking lives in war might actually save lives in the long run.

I don't remember now who realized it first, but at some point we came to the realization that we weren't really talking about two issues. We were talking about only one: Is it ever okay to kill? Is taking a life ever the lesser of two evils? Can killing ever be the moral choice? Once we saw that the conversation was about different circumstances within the same issue, we were able to let our defenses down. It wasn't that one of us valued life and the other didn't. It was just that each of us had a different set of circumstances where we felt killing could be justified.

That realization made our dialogue more open and friendly, and with that goal in mind I suggest that not only war and capital punishment, but also stem cell research, abortion, and euthanasia are also variants of the same question: Is it ever okay to kill? And while we're on the subject, I would be untrue to myself if I didn't suggest that the question should also be applied to the issues of hunting, protection of endangered species, and vegetarianism. I'm not proclaiming public policy on these issues, but advocating for more civil dialogue among Christians by finding the common root to our questions.

The Sixth Commandment

The sixth commandment is both perfectly clear and completely vague. In the Hebrew, there are only two words to the entire commandment. Don't kill. Every time the issue comes up, someone points out that "kill" is a bad translation that should have been rendered as "murder." That's true, as far as it goes. But I don't think God had American jurisprudence in mind in selecting the word.

We can get some sense of what "murder" meant to those who received the commandments by looking at the other places where that Hebrew word, *ratsach*, is used in Scripture. The premeditated slaughter of an innocent is presented in 1 Kings 21:19. Numbers 35:27 recounts the story of someone who kills out of vengeance. In Numbers 35:30 the word refers very specifically to vengeance by the community in capital punishment. The word is used for an accidental death in Joshua 20:3, for death by animal attack in Proverbs 22:13, and for acts of war in 2 Kings 6:32.

So the word *ratsach* in the commandment isn't as narrowly defined as some would like us to believe. "Murder" is as open to interpretation as "kill" is, even within the pages of the Bible. All of us tend to interpret this commandment in ways designed to keep ourselves out of the category of law breakers—or at least out of the category of people who approve of law breaking. In American society we seem to think that some commandments are more heinous to break than others, so we define "murder" narrowly, sentence the murderers to death, and promote the Sabbath breakers to company CEO.

Let's wade into the treacherous waters. Remember, this is only a book. If you're a diehard liberal and begin to reconsider your stance on abortion, relax. Nobody will know unless you tell them. And if you're head of the local pro-life organization and find yourself acknowledging that the issue is a bit muddier than it first seemed, realize that you are in a perfect position to build some bridges across a deep divide—and probably save some lives while you're at it. It's in the interest of all babies everywhere—both born and unborn—that Christians be able to have meaningful dialogue about how to kill less than we do. We also need ways to determine what constitutes "life," and what does not.

The Boundaries of Life

The debate around three major issues rises from our lack of certainty about what defines "life." Is a fetus a human being? How about a cell that could become a fetus? Is a brain-dead woman on life support alive? Some say "yes," others "no," and because life is as much spirit as science, we have a very hard time coming up with a definitive answer that will satisfy everyone.

Then there are the questions of quality. If a child about to be born is without brain function and destined to be on life support forever, is that really human life? If I'm in unbearable pain and the doctor says I'll die in a month anyway, can I end my suffering early? The questions are real, and we turn to the three issues that focus on the boundaries of life first: stem cell research, abortion, and euthanasia.

Stem Cell Research

I'd guess that many of the people who engage the debate don't know any more than I do about the biology and medicine involved, but stem cell research has ignited in the public sphere because no one seems sure whether or not using embryonic stem cells constitutes taking a life. Given that not everyone agrees that a fetus growing in a mother's womb is "alive" in any meaningful sense, it really shouldn't surprise us that we can't agree on an embryo in a petri dish.

So how do we come at this? The Bible doesn't even hint at this question, and if you can find a clear-cut answer to "What would Jesus do?" when confronted with an embryonic stem cell, you're a much more astute reader of Scripture than I. Rather than yelling at each other about this question, Christian theologians need to figure out what it means to be alive from a biblical point of view. Until we can reach a reasoned definition of life, taking into account both the revelation of Scripture and the revelation of science, we'll be stuck in our current mess, with partisan politics determining theology.

Here's what Scripture suggests to me about life: When I think about the origins of life, my brain jumps to Genesis and the creation of human beings in a two-step process. Consider, first, Genesis 2:7: "Then the Lord God formed man from the dust of the ground and breathed into his nostrils the breath of life; and the man became a living being." First God forms. God makes the body. But it's not until God breathes into his nostrils the breath of life that Adam is identified as a living being. Life in Genesis seems to be defined by both body and breath.

Oddly enough, if you're a Scriptural literalist, this doesn't leave room for even a ninth-month fetus to be alive, since it doesn't technically have breath until it exits the mother's womb. But we can be a bit broader and remember that the Hebrew word for "breath" here, *ruach*, means more than just the ability to take in oxygen. It's the word for wind, breath, and spirit. A person becomes "a living being" when God's spirit inhabits the earthly body.

We see this also in Ezekiel 37, in the story of the valley of dry bones. Ezekiel speaks God's word to the dry bones and we get the best Halloween story in the Bible. "Suddenly there was a noise, a rattling, and the bones came together, bone to its bone. I looked, and there were sinews on them, and flesh had come upon them, and skin had covered them; but there was no breath in them" (Ezek 37:7–8). Again we have step one: the formation of the body but absent the breath, the spirit, the *ruach*. The story goes on in verses 9 and 10: "Then he said to me, 'Prophesy to the breath, prophesy, mortal, and say to the breath: Thus says the Lord God: Come from the four winds, O breath, and breathe upon these slain, that they may live.' I prophesied as he commanded me, and the breath came into them, and they lived, and stood on their feet, a vast multitude."

Life in the Bible seems to be a two-step process: the formation of the body and the entering of the spirit, with the spirit being the final and determining factor. In both cases the spirit enters and gives life to the body and not the other way around, and in both cases, God provides that spirit. That says to me that life isn't something created by accident, but by God's intention.

Psalm 104 bears this out, as the psalmist talks about the dependence of all living things on God:

These all look to you
to give them their food in due season;
when you give to them, they gather it up;
when you open your hand, they are filled with good things.
When you hide your face, they are dismayed;
when you take away their breath, they die
and return to their dust.
When you send forth your spirit, they are created;
and you renew the face of the ground. (Psalm 104:27–30)

We've come to learn incredible things about the process God designed for the creation of the body. Even in the most sophisticated lab in the world, however, we don't have a clue about how to convey the mysterious *ruach*. Human beings seem close to learning how to create a fully formed human body, but we haven't moved an inch toward being able to make that form a living being. Still, like Ezekiel, we must call to the breath to give these forms life. The giving of life is still solely an act of God.

If you disagree with all of that, you'll have to find your own way through the maze of these issues. I don't know how to help you. But if you agree that God is the giver of life, and that there can be bodies that are not living beings, there seems to be at least some room for saying that an embryo (and perhaps even some stages of a fetus) might not yet be filled with that life-giving spirit.

This is where some of the other things we believe about God come into play. If you believe that God has every moment of every person's life figured out ahead of time, then do you honestly think God will put that spirit into an embryo specifically created for research or a fetus that God knows will be aborted? That doesn't sound like the God I know. For my part, I don't believe God has everything figured out ahead of time (that discussion will have to wait for another book), but I very much believe in God's intentionality and God's love. That means that I come out in a very similar place, but for different reasons.

God has clearly allowed us to know some things (how bodies are formed) and not others (how and when the spirit enters, or even what that means). If God has allowed us to figure out things about bodily formation, then perhaps discovering stem cells and their medical use was part of what God intended for us to combat disease and better love our neighbors through healing. If God has been intentional about keeping secret the process that actually confers "life," so that a person first "lives" only by God's intention, then maybe we can quit worrying that we have accidentally created "life" in a petri dish when we only meant to create a collection of cells.

There may be some fatal theological flaw in that argument, or perhaps other portions of Scripture that I haven't considered might result in a completely different view. I don't mean to say that this is the only way Christians can view stem cell research, abortion, or anything else. But these are the sorts of discussions that Christians and ethicists ought to be having rather than polarized debates where each side thinks the other is the devil.

I'm concerned that the Christians who I hear debating the issue of embryonic stem cell research have cut out the actions of God just as much as scientists often do. There seems to be the assumption that life is created automatically when certain physical functions have occurred. That's perfectly understandable for those who don't profess belief in a creator God. But for Christians that stance is a lapse in faith. For us, God is the author of life, as much involved in the process today as on day six of creation. For us, God hasn't abandoned the world to mechanical and biological processes, although God works in and through those to great effect. I'm concerned that Christians sometimes talk as if science and biology are the authors of life, and forget that God has held back a part of the life-giving process from our knowledge. God still holds the knowledge of the secret ingredient—the *ruach*—and if God is still in control of life, maybe we can relax enough to deal sensibly with the issue.

Abortion

If there's one issue in this country with which we seem unable to relax and deal sensibly, it's abortion. Once we take the embryo out of a dish and find it planted securely in a mother's womb, the question of when that *ruach* enters becomes even more difficult. Add in the emotions of the mother who is very literally bonding with that fetus, ultrasonic pictures that allow us to determine a gender, see movement, and detect abnormalities, and we have a volatile mix. I should start by admitting my own bias, and go from there. For my part, I think abortion should be both unthinkable and legal, although the latter seems to me more like the lesser of two evils than a true good. With the possible exception of something as quick as the "morning after pill," I have a feeling that many, if not most, abortions are the taking of a life.

I remember being very startled in seminary when I read a study on abortion, with interviews of women who'd terminated their pregnancies. Almost every one of them considered it murder. I was a pretty staunch pro-lifer at the time, and I'd spent all of my energies trying to shout to the world that abortion was murder, thinking that if people just realized that, abortions would stop. When I read that most of the women thought it was murder to begin with, I was stunned. I had the issue all wrong. The issue, at least for those getting abortions, wasn't whether it was murder or not but whether, in their particular situations, the murder was justified.

It's hard for me to put myself in the shoes of a woman who has an abortion. Throughout my late twenties and early thirties, I struggled with the growing realization that I couldn't bear children. I had more tests than I care to talk about, and no one ever found out what the problem was, but no child was ever able to grow in my womb. That's a terribly painful blow to a woman, and I spent many a year unable to deal with Mother's Day, infant baptisms, and baby showers. Since I wanted children so badly and couldn't have them, it's hard for me to put myself in the position of a woman who ends her pregnancy.

But I've seen some circumstances that have helped me to understand. Pastoral ministry has allowed me to see, up close and personal, into the underside of society. I've known girls who were pregnant with their father's baby—a baby who, when born, would be raped too. I've known young women whose boyfriends have threatened to kill them if they don't abort the baby because they don't want to be responsible for child support payments. And I've known the boyfriends well enough to know the threats were real.

I've also seen the women who didn't have abortions, whose children live in squalor and neglect or who die at the hands of abusive caretakers. I've seen new mothers who are emotionally, financially, and mentally unfit to care for special-needs children they didn't abort but now can't help. And I've seen those who convinced her to have the child because abortion would be terribly wrong melt into the woodwork when the child is born, offering only guilt if there is an abortion and not a shred of help when the child arrives.

Once when I lived in a strong pro-life community, I spoke with those organizing a pro-life rally. I suggested that in addition to making the statement that abortion was wrong, we might turn the event into a pro-life fair, with adoption agencies and a booth with counselors. We could invite those who oppose abortion to sign up as foster parents, as volunteers with day-care facilities or any of the social service agencies that try to help mothers raise children in difficult circumstances. "We could really give some options and some hope," I said, "rather than just making people feel guilty for taking the only road they feel able to manage." Of course none of that happened. The rally was held, and those who came just gathered along the streets with signs condemning abortion, those who have them, and those who perform them. It didn't seem helpful to me.

I've also seen women on their second or third abortion—those who scatter their sexuality like seed and would rather undergo a surgical procedure than endure the consequences of their actions. I believe that needs to stop.

Because I have seen precious young women—even girls—in simply impossible circumstances, I shudder at the thought of a hard and fast law that would send those already abused to a dark alley with a coat hanger. I want those girls to at least have a sterile environment and caring staff as they go through the physical and emotional turmoil of abortion. That makes me vote to keep abortion legal. But that doesn't mean I wish for a world where abortion happens. I want us to care enough about the poor and the abused to create systems where no woman is forced to choose between her own life and the life of her unborn child. I want us to be sure our laws don't cut off the poor at the knees on the one hand but do have severe consequences for abortion as birth control on the other.

Mostly I want us to stop acting like toddlers when we talk to each other about this. I want pro-lifers to quit calling me a baby killer when I vote against laws that would save a baby but kill a mom. And I want the pro-choice folks to quit saying that those who oppose Roe v. Wade hate women and want to send us back to the dark ages. There's a fanatical fringe to every issue, but most of us actually agree on the basics. We all think life is sacred, but we differ on when we think it begins. We all want fewer abortions. None of us think murder is a fine thing. We just differ in whether making abortion illegal will help or harm the cause of life and liberty for all.

Euthanasia

All the issues so far, including this one, have two things in common: they deal with questions surrounding the boundaries of life, and the Bible doesn't talk directly about any of them. That leaves us with the difficult job of trying to apply biblical principles to new situations, as we decide what a Christian response to euthanasia looks like.

I confess that the question of assisted suicide is something that makes me want to hide. We have recently put my mother in a nursing home. The fog of Alzheimer's has been so swift and so relentless that I barely adjust to one reality before the situation changes again. What will I wish for her when she's curled up in a fetal position, unable to recognize her own daughter? What was it like in the hidden places of her spirit when she heard the doctor's diagnosis and knew what lay in store? All she said to me of the doctor's pronouncement was, "I wish she had said something else."

I'd unplug her from a machine in a heartbeat, knowing that when Death comes, he'll come not with a scythe but with a shepherd's crook—the gentle friend she's loved all her life. I'd take away artificial means of prolonging a vegetative or suffering life and view that death as a gift. But would I use artificial means to end it? Would I authorize an injection or a pill to end her life before her body deemed it necessary? That's the question I don't want to face. I can barely face it with the dog, let alone my mother. How does a Christian respond?

What biblical principles can speak to the desire to end our lives or the lives of others in great suffering? Well, we sing, "They'll know we are Christians by our love," and that's as good a place as any to start. The Bible is clear that "God is love" (1 John 4:8b) and Paul makes it clear in 1 Corinthians 13 that love trumps everything else—even faith. So, can assisted suicide be a loving act?

I wish that question were as simple to answer as it is to ask. On the one hand, the person asking for an end to life is asking for mercy and compassion, two of the many faces of love. They want release and relief and an end to their suffering. If my mother were begging that from me, I think I'd either melt into a puddle on the floor or take the pill myself.

But part of the reason I'm conflicted is that we seem to respond differently to physical suffering than we do to emotional suffering, though they can be equal in their intensity and effects. When people come to me consumed with mental anguish to the point of wanting to take their own lives, I haven't helped them load the gun, pop the pills, or find a razor blade, much as I loved them and wanted their suffering to end. That hasn't even crossed my mind. I have called 911.

Aside from the fact that I'm mandated by law to do that, there are theological reasons for my actions. One of them is the complex relationship that Christian faith has with suffering. We are the ones who claim a suffering, crucified Messiah as Lord and Savior. We are the spiritual descendants of the martyrs and the mystics who prayed day and night to be worthy to suffer with Christ. We are the ones who have answered the call to take up a cross and follow Jesus. Accepting an easy out from the ravages of life seems somehow less than what we are called to be.

Every Lent we remind ourselves that the people of God were formed in the wilderness. Every Good Friday we look brutality and suffering square in the face and, with an inner confidence say, "Ah, but this is not the end of the story." We are the ones who proclaim every Easter that God is capable of taking the worst suffering human beings can endure and using it to save the world. I know ministers are supposed to understand all this, but I have to admit that I don't. Suffering seems to be part of the overall plan, and that is first on my list of things to ask God about one day. I would have followed a Messiah who was skipping through poppy fields . . . really. But that doesn't seem to be God's way.

While we're called to alleviate the suffering of others, we're also supposed to embrace the natural suffering of life. This paradoxical approach to suffering has been greatly misused. The next time I hear a Christian say that someone should endure beatings by a spouse in order to suffer with Christ, I'll forget I am a Christian for a moment and do some damage.

But I also will never forget a story I heard about a young man who was a home nurse for a man who could move no part of his body except his eyes. The nurse was telling about how he learned to interpret what the man wanted and needed through his eyes, but the culmination of the story was that the nurse gave his life to Christ as a result of learning about love through that man.

When I think of those who wish to end their lives because of their suffering, that story comes to mind, and I find I have to ask the painful question, "Suppose it isn't about me after all?" Even though that invalid didn't have a shred of what we normally think of as "quality of life," someone else found God in the process of caring for him. If I've given my life over to God, is it really for me to determine that God can have no further use of it? Is the world centered on my comfort? Shall I say, "This time, God, it's my will, not yours"?

Some people say that knowing they have the option of assisted suicide gives them the courage to face another day. I understand that. Knowing we have choices, however difficult they are, provides a sense of true power. In many ways we're better equipped to make the right choices when we don't feel trapped or coerced. And while I think Christian faith teaches us to put our suffering into God's hands rather than take it into our own, I'm pretty uncomfortable in demanding through law that others do so, regardless of their own faith and circumstances. So, I think I would vote to make legal something I believe would be wrong for myself. I'm not sure how, but I think that once we've pledged our lives to the Crucified One, we should follow him to the end. I just intend to keep praying hard that such a cup will pass from me!

Killing as an Act of the State

Capital Punishment

For ten years I lived in and around Gainesville, Florida, a town not far from Stark, the home of "Old Sparky," Florida's now retired electric chair. During the time that I lived there, Ted Bundy was executed and Danny Rolling terrorized Gainesville with his string of University of Florida student murders. A friend's little daughter stopped eating her cereal during those months, thinking that would somehow fend off the serial (cereal) killer. It was an anxious time. It was also a time that struck close to home as the niece of our church organist became one of the victims, her head chopped off and put on a shelf facing the door to create a memorable image for whoever was first on the scene.

Also during that time I was engaged in volunteer literacy work in the prisons, training maximum security inmates to be tutors for other inmates who couldn't read. I had an active correspondence with sixteen lifers and heard the stories from both sides. There seemed to be a constant effort to write the governor and request that life sentences be commuted to death sentences, so there'd be a light at the end of the tunnel—an end to their prison stay. I heard of inmates who wished their crimes had been a bit more heinous so that they could have their fifteen minutes of fame as a death-row inmate and then have their wretched lives ended.

At an ecumenical church service I met the mother of an inmate on death row. She sat with me for awhile as we shared refreshments, sobbing with the agony of knowing that the state was determined to kill her son, and I wondered who was really receiving the punishment. A man in my own church was one of the corrections officers at the Stark prison, charged with flipping the switch on Old Sparky. All these things have made me wonder.

Of course there are unsettling statistics. The following points come from the Death Penalty Information Center in Washington, DC:

- There are 38 states that have the death penalty, with 1,029 executions (22 for crimes committed as juveniles) since 1976. Of that 1,029, 861 were executed by lethal injection, 152 by electrocution, 11 in the gas chamber, 3 by hanging, and 2 by firing squad.
- Since 1973 over 120 people have been released from death row with evidence of their innocence.
- In 96 percent of the states where there have been reviews of race and the death penalty, there was a pattern of either race-of-victim or race-of-defendant discrimination, or both.
- A survey of the former and present presidents of the country's top academic criminological societies showed that 84 percent rejected the notion that the death penalty acts as a deterrent to murder.[1]

The evidence appears to be that the death penalty doesn't deter crime, has the potential to execute the innocent, and is tainted by racial prejudice. And then there's the company we keep. Neither our North American neighbors (with the exception of Cuba) nor our European or Scandinavian allies have the death penalty. Instead, we sit in the company of Iraq, Iran, Saudi Arabia, Uganda, China, and Libya.

The evidence of racial injustice in the application of the death penalty should concern us as Christians, as should the execution of the innocent. But the question is broader than simply worrying that we are executing the innocent. Jesus called us to love our enemies as well as the innocent.

As Christians, let's ask, "On what basis do we decide that a life is beyond God's redeeming?" Part of the reason I support legalized abortion is that I think making it illegal won't stop the procedure; it will just make it more dangerous. In capital punishment, however, we're dealing with a population already under the direct control of the state. They are not going to die anyway, except at the end of their natural lives.

The attitudes in the Christian community around this issue baffle me. This is a place where all those folks with "What would Jesus do?" bracelets hide them under their sleeves and forget the New Testament, as though God never acted past Deuteronomy and as if the Levitical laws calling for execution for a whole variety of crimes are still in play. Of course, those people are not advocating adherence to those specific laws (except when it comes to homosexuality), since killing a child for being strong-willed seems a bit harsh to us (Deut 21:18–21), but the Mosaic Law allows for capital punishment, so our doing so becomes "biblical."

Jesus wasn't confronted with the abortion issue, as far as we know. He did, however, have direct input into a capital case; you can read about it in John 8 when the people bring to him a woman caught in adultery. The law says to stone her. It is a capital offense, and the case is given over to Jesus for judgment. Jesus shows his brilliance. He knows they want to snag him by having him blatantly disregard the law. They know he has a bleeding-heart reputation, and seems far too tolerant toward sin for any respectable rabbi. They want to bring him down, and he knows it.

He also knows the human heart, and here he uses that knowledge to his advantage. "Let anyone among you who is without sin be the first to throw a stone at her." Brilliant. He acknowledges that sin deserves punishment as stated in the law. But he also shows that, when it comes to breaking God's law, human beings have no business talking in "us and them" terms. We've all sinned, and the greater law of justice is threatened when we decide that the sins of others are worse than our own. All the would-be stoners walk away, leaving only Jesus. Jesus lets her off. "'Woman, where are they? Has no one condemned you?' She said, 'No one, sir.' And Jesus said, 'Neither do I condemn you. Go your way, and from now on do not sin again.'" He doesn't say it wasn't sin. He doesn't say it doesn't matter. But he does ensure that she doesn't die for her sin.

"Turn the other cheek," "Put away your swords," "Father, forgive them. They don't know what they're doing." How come those who insist we follow the mandates of the Bible don't find those words of Jesus applicable to the case of capital punishment? Is it possible that Jesus suffered capital punishment so others wouldn't have to?

And what does the execution of a death-row inmate do to us as a society? I remember the Ted Bundy execution. The atmosphere outside the prison was like a carnival. Placards read "Fry, Bundy, fry!" and there was true delight in the moment of his death. Now, on the one hand, I understand that. I know from the dark places of my own soul the desire for vengeance, and the hope that others will suffer in the same ways they caused suffering for their victims. But I also know those feelings to be less than Jesus has called me to be.

Where in Scripture does it tell us to rejoice in the destruction of our enemies? The prophet Obadiah says in verse 12: "But you should not have gloated over your brother on the day of his misfortune; you should not have rejoiced over the people of Judah on the day of their ruin; you should not have boasted on the day of distress." Does anybody honestly think that Jesus rejoiced on the day of Ted Bundy's execution?

It seems to me that God says "Vengeance is mine" not only because God is better equipped to make a true judgment, but also because giving free reign to vengeance does harm to the human soul. We all rest a bit easier when a dangerous person can no longer inflict harm, but to rejoice in a death makes us a little less human. God gave life to Ted Bundy. Ted Bundy was an innocent baby once. God had hopes and dreams and plans for his life: hopes for a positive life, a life devoted to God and to good. But Ted Bundy misused his freedom. He abused the life that God gave him and stole the life that God had given to others.

I believe God was horrified at what Bundy did and that God cried with the families of every life that Bundy ended. But I also believe that God cried the night that Ted Bundy was electrocuted—for a life gone bad, a soul lost in the depths of evil. I believe that God wished it might have been different; I do not believe that God danced.

It may be that my friend Veronica is right. It might be that the only way to truly protect society is to end the lives of certain people. For myself, I can't go there. I think there's too great a chance that we'll execute the innocent. Far from being a deterrent, I think it actually makes some people bolster their crimes to attain the death penalty as a status. I think life in prison is actually a worse punishment, and that a death sentence punishes the family. And when I ask the question "What would Jesus do?" I can't see him flipping the switch.

But surely we can all agree that the death of anyone is a time for tears, not rejoicing. Surely we can stand outside death-row prisons with bowed heads and candles rather than cheers and popcorn. During the time I lived in Florida there was a re-election campaign for the governor. One of the TV commercials boasted of the number of death warrants the governor had signed during his first term. Father, forgive them. They don't know what they're doing.

War

To sign a declaration of war is to sign death warrants for, at the very least, thousands of innocent people. It's also signing death warrants for some guilty ones, but war is far less precise than capital punishment, and those who think the innocent are spared in war have never come close to its horrors. Because of that, war is never something to be entered into lightly or quickly or without the certainty that the lives taken in war will be fewer than the lives lost without one.

The Bible, of course, would be a much shorter book if it weren't for war. God's people are always either marching out to war or being marched upon themselves, often, we're told, at the direction of God. One segment of Scripture says that God will see to it that our swords are beaten into plowshares and our spears into pruning hooks (Isa 2:4); but another passage says exactly the opposite (Joel 3:10). Jesus tells the disciples in one place to put away their swords, warning that those who live by the sword will die by it (Matt 26:52) and then in another place instructs them to sell something so that they can buy a sword to take with them (Luke 22:36).

When Jesus talks about the end times, he says there will be war. "Nation will rise against nation" (Matt 24:7) and it seems that Jesus sees war as inevitable on the earth. Revelation even tells us that there is war in heaven (Rev 12:7), something that caught me up short when I realized it. By the end of the book of Revelation it seems that both heaven and earth have become so tainted that new ones of both are in order. "Then I saw a new heaven and a new earth; for the first heaven and the first earth had passed away, and the sea was no more" (Rev 21:1). We are told in this new universe that "He will wipe every tear from their eyes. Death will be no more; mourning and crying and pain will be no more, for the first things have passed away" (Rev 21:4).

All of this tells me two things. First, that the old question from the sixties, "What if they had a war and nobody came?" may be a theoretical peace plan, but while we're here in the midst of these "first things," it's not a terribly likely scenario. As the old Pete Seeger song claimed, flowers will go to young girls who will go to young men who will go to soldiers who will go to graveyards who will go to flowers for a long time yet to come. When will they ever learn? The Bible seems to indicate that they won't . . . even in heaven.

Secondly, however, I think the Bible is equally clear that war isn't an act of goodness in God's eyes. King David, the shepherd-turned-warrior, isn't allowed to build God's temple because of the blood on his hands. "But the word of the Lord came to me, saying, 'You have shed much blood and have waged great wars; you shall not build a house to my name, because you have shed so much blood in my sight on the earth'" (1 Chr 22:8). Never mind that the Bible records that God told him to engage many of those wars, it has tainted him nonetheless. War may be necessary in a given instance, but it's still not the way God intended the world to be. It might be the lesser of two evils, but it's clearly not a "good."

We see this even more plainly when God comes to earth in human form, showing us what God's perfect will looks like living in our world. The people of Israel in the first century look to Jesus to rise up and lead them in a war to overthrow the Romans. This was their expectation for a Messiah, and there's every reason for them to want it. The oppression of the occupying Roman force was brutal. The Romans took their money, their resources, and on at least one occasion slaughtered all the children under two years old in the city. But Jesus rejected that road to liberty, taking the violence into himself on the cross instead. There's no indication that Jesus ever carried a weapon. Paul calls Jesus the pioneer and perfecter of our faith (Heb 12:2), and I think the pacifism of Jesus is one of the ways that Jesus set the example and blazed a new trail.

At the end, though, the Bible tells us, when these "first things" have passed away, God's dream will come to pass. Heaven and earth will be re-created and both will be free of death and mourning and crying and pain. There will be no more war in heaven or on earth when God's will is truly done. A world with no war is the dream of God. The life of Jesus shows what happens to the pacifist in this world, and so it has ever been. Those who refuse to go to war are labeled traitors; those who oppose any given war are called unpatriotic, and in many cultures throughout history, they have been slaughtered because of their work to achieve peace without violence. Read the history of the Crusades or the Anabaptists, if you doubt it. Remember the damaging rhetoric of Vietnam or Iraq; remember Martin Luther King, Jr. and Mahatma Gandhi.

I don't understand why pacifists are so hated, or how they can be maligned by those who profess to be Christians. Even if we differ on whether or not a particular war is necessary, we ought to at least recognize that the pacifist represents the dream of God and the dream of all people—a world free from the ravages of war. When I pray the Lord's Prayer and say, "Thy kingdom come, thy will be done," I'm praying, among other things, for all that the pacifist stands for to come upon the earth: the end of all wars, the cessation of violence, the obliteration of every weapon.

If I want my country to be a land where the will of God is done, I want to see great reluctance and mourning over a decision to go to war. I want to know that fewer of God's children will die with that war than without it, and that every precaution has been taken to treat our enemies with as much dignity as possible, whether or not the law requires it. That doesn't come from my politics but from my faith, which tells me that God's dream for our world is loving our enemies, and that when God's will is done on earth, "they shall beat their swords into plowshares and their spears into pruning hooks; nation shall not lift up sword against nation, neither shall they learn war anymore" (Isa 2:4).

Non-Human Life

It may seem ridiculous to talk about the taking of animal life in the same chapter as serious matters like war and abortion. Some don't consider animals at all, apart from their usefulness to human beings . . . bomb sniffing dogs, laboratory mice, winning race horses, chickens that end up on our dinner plates, and deer that we can hunt.

This isn't, however, the biblical view. The Law of Moses, including the Ten Commandments, had provisions for animals as well as human beings. We looked at this some when we talked about Sabbath. It's true that there's a hierarchy of life in Scripture, with people placed above the animals, but the "dominion" given to human beings isn't modeled on the dominion of a tyrannical king over his subjects but on the rule of God. It's leadership with the goal that all within the kingdom flourish and thrive in the love of God.

In the church we call this stewardship. The animals are given to us in trust, to tend until the day of accounting, when God will ask how the sixth day of creation treated the five days that came before it. Last I checked, the cattle on a thousand hills still belonged to God: "I will not accept a bull from your house, or goats from your folds. For every wild animal of the forest is mine, the cattle on a thousand hills. I know all the birds of the air, and all that moves in the field is mine" (Ps 50:9–11). If you think God doesn't care about how we treat God's creatures, we're reading different Bibles.

Hunting

Once upon a time, anthropologists tell us, human beings were hunter-gatherers—the women stayed home, picked herbs for medicines or berries for food, and tended the hearth and children. The men went out to kill some animals for food, clothing, and often for many household objects or commodities. In some parts of the world, life still operates this way, and I believe that this is what hunting is for. Jesus didn't condemn his fishermen disciples for catching live fish to feed themselves and their communities—he even helped them do it.

Hunting as sport, however, is an entirely different matter. Violent video games are condemned for encouraging violence, but we have a national industry devoted to real-life killing as a sport. Both candidates in the 2004 presidential election had to prove that they enjoyed going out in the woods to kill God's creatures for any chance of being elected.

Killing and sport don't belong together. What message does that send to our children? Is that teaching them their role of stewards of God's earth? Never mind that much of what passes for hunting isn't even sportsmanlike. Baiting the animals? Making them think you're a friend so you can blow their brains out? Tying a tiger to a tree and suspending yourself from a cage so you can shoot the savage beast and mount it at your summer camp? Shooting wolves from planes and helicopters? You call that sport?

I've heard the argument: "We have to shoot the deer or the herds will get too large for the food supply and starve!" God thought of that, you know, and gave us the larger predators—wolves and mountain lions. But in many areas where predator reintroduction has been proposed, hunters are strongly opposed because balancing the ecosystem would take away their sport. There are economic issues, too—aerial hunters pay a hefty price for their sport, and though it's illegal no one stops them—it's far too lucrative an industry.

I question the sincerity of those hunters who express concern about deer overpopulation and the strength of the herd. I question it because I have yet to see a diseased fawn head mounted proudly on anyone's wall. Maybe those folks are just quieter about it, but all the hunters I know (and there are some who are dear friends of mine) want the strong buck, not the weakest link. Natural predators both thin the herd and strengthen it by taking its weakest members. It's survival of the fittest at its prime. Human hunters weaken the overall herd by taking its strongest and best.

In my wildest dreams I cannot imagine that God ever intended human beings to make killing into sport. John Wesley, the founder of the Methodist movement, spoke out vehemently against the cock fighting and animal abuses of his day. He also preached a sermon called "The General Deliverance" reminding us of the Romans 8 passage that tells us all of creation, and not just human beings, are part of God's redemption.

Yes, Jesus says that we are worth more than many sparrows (Matt 10:31), but just a few verses before that, he says that the Father knows about every sparrow that falls (Matt 10:29). Genesis 9:5 says that animals will be held accountable for shedding the blood of a human, but I don't believe people will be found guiltless for killing God's creatures for fun. According to the Bible, "the earth is the Lord's and all that is in it" (Ps 24:1).

The issue isn't limited to cute, furry animals—Christians shouldn't stomp on ants for fun any more than I believe we should shoot five-point bucks for fireplace decorations. I don't find biblical support for taking delight in killing anything, and if we manage to make sport of stomping on ants, we may find that we have opened a cancer in our souls that will spread. It might start small, but the bloodlust will grow, as human history shows. Once we forget that one thing belongs to God, it's easier to forget the next thing. Instead of calling them God's creatures, we begin to justify our actions by calling them "pests." It creeps up the food chain.

First it's the ants at the picnic, then it's the mice who chewed my boat cover. Then it's the blue jays who don't have pretty voices and take all the seed from the "nice" birds. Next we have to eliminate the Canada geese because they interfere with our golf game, and the woodchucks because they enjoy the food we planted on top of their homes. And so on, up the food chain, until the "pest" is me, or you.

Call me a crazy extremist. I believe that's how it works. I think it is a gradual move of forgetfulness and carelessness that goes unnoticed because we have become so calloused toward them. Maybe if we stopped using the words "pest," "animal," and "beast," and started calling all living things "God's creatures," we could start to remember our role here on earth. I'm not trying to say that it is never appropriate to kill an animal. But Christians should remember that the animal they want to kill belongs to God, and it is only common courtesy to check with the owner before you do it in.

There's not much time for prayerful communication when a panther is dropping on you from a nearby tree branch, and I have a feeling God would forgive you that shot as an act of self-defense. But just what would you say if God showed up beside you some Saturday when you are out in the woods with your gun and said, "So, whatchya doin'?" "My children are starving, and I need to bring them food," is a pretty good answer. "A mountain lion has carried off my wife," would probably find a sympathetic hearing. "I am so horrified by the way that your creatures are kept on factory farms that I prefer to get meat more naturally," would probably even get God to take notes. I'm not so sure that "I wanted to find something I could shoot and hang on my wall" would be as welcome.

Eating Meat

I eat meat. This is hypocritical because if I had to kill the cow or the chicken myself, I'd forswear meat forever. But, in my cowardice, I allow others to do it for me and eat the results. It's not just cowardice; it's also laziness. I live a stressed-out, busy life; I hate to cook and hate grocery shopping even more. My meals at home are pretty much restricted to what I can open and consume on the spot. On the plus side, meat requires planning and preparation so I don't cook it very often. Meals for me tend to be cottage cheese and applesauce, and in the mornings I go all out and toast a bagel. It's not a balanced diet, and every so often my body tells me it wants something more substantial, so I go out and get dinner, and I eat meat.

The biblical record is a mixed bag on this. The creation account in Genesis 1:30 says that God made everything vegetarian. "And to every beast of the earth, and to every bird of the air, and to everything that creeps on the earth, everything that has the breath of life, I have given every green plant for food." Apparently in God's initial design, there either were no carnivores or the creatures we now know as carnivores had other tastes.

All this changes after the story of Noah—an ironic twist. After being included in God's great act of salvation, all the animals gratefully plant their paws back on terra firma and overhear God saying to Noah and his family, "Every moving thing that lives shall be food for you; and just as I gave you the green plants, I give you everything" (Gen 9:3). I can just hear the rabbits now, "Every moving thing shall be food . . . Moving things . . . I'm not moving. Are you moving, Harold? No, siree, no movement over here. . . . "

Right after the introduction of meat-eating comes the first law about not eating blood, and the notice that even the animals will have to give a reckoning for human life. As the Old Testament progresses there are more and more laws about food in general and meat in particular. The pronouncement to Noah was that it was okay to eat any moving thing, but by the time of the Mosaic Law, lots of moving things had been ruled out as unclean. The means of preparing meat were detailed, and meat-eating, in general, had gotten much more complicated.

We know Jesus ate fish, and since he celebrated Passover, we can pretty well assume he ate lamb, but Daniel and his companions (Dan 1:8–17) insist on being given only vegetables and water as rations, which God blesses. And Paul in Romans 14:2 says, "Some believe in eating anything, while the weak eat only vegetables."

Biblically, I think the best advice comes from Paul in that fourteenth chapter of the book of Romans, especially as it is summed up in verses 19–23:

> Let us then pursue what makes for peace and for mutual upbuilding. Do not, for the sake of food, destroy the work of God. Everything is indeed clean, but it is wrong for you to make others fall by what you eat; it is good not to eat meat or drink wine or do anything that makes your brother or sister stumble. The faith that you have, have as your own conviction before God. Blessed are those who have no reason to condemn themselves because of what they approve. But those who have doubts are condemned if they eat, because they do not act from faith; for whatever does not proceed from faith is sin.

Paul is saying that we should be mindful and intentional in why we eat what we eat, for all we do we should do to the glory of God. If I eat meat, I should be mindful that God has provided it and thank God for the gift.

I've always been fond of the Native American practice of thanking the animal that gave its life for their food. That seems right, somehow, even though I doubt the cow on my plate volunteered for the position. If I abstain from meat, I should do so thanking God that there are other healthy things to eat that don't involve taking a life. In both cases, I should try not to be a stumbling block to those who have reached a different conclusion. I think that whole chapter of Romans 14 is the most help of any on this issue.

We also should carefully think through why we do what we do. One of the reasons I am so conflicted over my consumption of meat is that

I know the abominable conditions under which factory farm animals are kept. I haven't yet been able to move to a meat-free diet, but I do try to buy chicken products that are cage-free, and I'd pay more for a steak in a restaurant that would guarantee that the beef came from a farm where cows grazed contented and free until their final day. When I eat pork, I am as distressed at the deplorable conditions that this pig had to endure to become my dinner as I am about the fact that it lost its life. If the meat industry wants to keep me in its carnivorous ranks, it had better work toward humane farming.

I run into this issue every time I teach a Bible study that covers the sacrificial system of ancient Israel. At a single festival, tens of thousands of animals would be slaughtered at the altar. I could hardly think about it, until one time a student said to me, "So you think slaughterhouses are better?" Suddenly I got a new perspective. Most of the time, the animal sacrifices were consumed by either the Levites or the family that brought the sacrifice. The fat and some of the other parts were burned and then the rest was eaten. The sacrifice was how most families got their meat.

When I thought about the way they got their meat and the way I got mine, I had to admit that theirs was preferable. In both cases the animal is slaughtered, but at least in the Israelite system it was done as an act of thankful worship. Meat-eating was so tied to religious observance that by Paul's day it had become a problem because you had to be sure that your meat had not come from a sacrifice to a pagan god. That's the trouble spurring the Romans 14 chapter. The Christians didn't know whether it was okay to eat meat if they weren't sure where it came from. Paul sets them straight—it's the attitude with which we eat, not the substance of our eating that determines sin.

In my own life I need to either stop sobbing over the chicken on my plate or learn to like cooking and shopping. But all of us can be more mindful in our eating. We can be more careful to thank God for what's on our plate, and learn to honor any life that was given in order to feed us. Once we can talk about honoring a life that was given for us, maybe we can get serious about reforming our farms, our slaughterhouses and our attitudes about our relationship to God's creatures. In the meantime, Paul reminds us, all creation is groaning for its redemption.

7

Be Faithful

Thou shalt not commit adultery.

Whenever I preach a sermon series on the Ten Commandments, "adultery Sunday" is always well-attended. You don't have to look very far or very hard in American culture to find examples of the sin of adultery and of our fascination with it. Unfortunately, you don't even have to look outside of the church walls.

As I write these words, I periodically stop to check my e-mail, trying to keep in touch with two friends whose marriage is coming to a heartbreaking end. It's a textbook case, really. Like so many others, a loving young couple grew apart, didn't communicate their needs, and then one of them began to fill those needs outside the marriage. The betrayed spouse is devastated, the children are fearful, and the straying spouse is too caught up in the rapture of new love to realize how needless and destructive and harmful it is.

I wish it were only an occasional problem, but adultery is no respecter of persons. Men do it. Women do it. It happens in gay and lesbian relationships as well as heterosexual relationships. It visits families across racial, cultural, and economic lines. It visits the church, the academy, and the courtroom. It visited my life and ended a ten-year marriage. My mother was abandoned at four years of age when her mother ran off with another man. In one church I served there was so much of it that I wanted to stand up in the pulpit and say, "Okay, is there anyone here this morning who is actually sleeping with the person they're supposed to be sleeping with? Anybody at all?" I really wouldn't have expected many hands to go up. Sometimes I wish I knew the congregations I serve a little less well.

My own observation has led me down some interesting roads. It's easy just to shake a finger and say, "Bad adulterer! Hang your head in shame!" But I think that ignores the complexity of the issue. I run into people who see nothing wrong with what they're doing. Exclude the predator just bent on sexual conquest for a moment. There are a host of other folks who are genuinely good people—Christian, even. For one reason or another they've allowed themselves to fall in love with someone outside their marriage and now that new person is meeting their emotional and sexual needs. They believe those needs can't be met—or can't be met as well—by their covenant partner, and it seems that the choice before them is either satisfaction or despair.

That's a hard place to be, and from that place the Christian brain drifts to some natural thoughts: "God doesn't want me to be unhappy." "God is love and this new relationship is loving, so God must approve." "No one will be hurt if it stays secret." Most are not bad people, they just are missing some key information.

What I think is missing, at least in the churches I'm familiar with, is a solid theology of marriage and sexuality. American culture, and especially American Christian culture, is so neurotic about sexual issues that we can hardly deal with the topic like mature adults. So we tend not to deal with it at all, except in childlike terms of good and bad. Even in families, we shy away. My own mother ended the "birds and bees" discussion with me when we finished the book called *A Doctor Talks to 9- to 12-year-olds*. She just couldn't talk about anything past puberty. A thirteen-year-old girl in one of the churches I served came to me to ask basic sex questions that her mother had told her she didn't need to know. In most cases, what we know about sexuality and committed relationships comes not from the church, but from the popular culture around us.

Despite the fact that sexual issues are tearing apart almost every Christian denomination, if Christian theologians are doing much of anything in the area of the theology of sexuality and commitment, it's not finding its way into the churches. In forty-five years of church-going, I've heard little that's more profound than a recital of "Thou shalt nots." Maybe that works for some people, but I know a whole lot of folks for whom such commandments carry little moral authority . . . except of course when they want to use them to condemn others.

I don't think we can reasonably expect to solve the adultery problem by proclaiming our condemnation either more frequently or more loudly. The problem is not ignorance of the commandment. The problem, I think, is ignorance of God's purpose in marriage. If we knew what God was thinking back on that sixth day when God created them male and female (Gen 1:27) and proclaimed that they should come together and become one flesh (Gen 2:24) maybe we could begin to get a handle on the purpose behind our sexuality and covenant relationships—relationships that are forged in promise and commitment both to each other and to a higher ideal.

For complicated reasons, personal sexual expressions tend to become public issues. So we will deal with it all . . . from the more personal side of adultery and faithfulness, divorce and sexual preference, to the more socially oriented issues of pornography, prostitution, and sex trafficking. But first, the foundation.

Marriage and Relationships

I am no expert on wedded bliss. I had a marriage that ended in divorce after ten years and an enormous mistake that ended with a legal annulment after only seven months. I don't pretend to be able to tell anybody how to have an exciting and fulfilling marriage that will last fifty years, although I can catalogue the critical mistakes made in relationships pretty accurately. I don't approach this chapter from the moral high ground.

I offer the thoughts and ideas of someone who has struggled with the nature and purpose of Christian marriage, both to help the relationships of the people I serve and to give myself a more secure foundation so that I can be smarter in my own.

On my journey to figure out the mystery of marriage—and why I couldn't seem to have one that worked—I noticed that Christian faith is fundamentally about relationships of all kinds. At the center of Christian faith is not a doctrine or a creed, but a person offering relationship. A God who decides to enter human history to restore an intimate and personal relationship with human beings is where it all begins. Relationship is central to our faith.

I began to think about Bible passages and wondered how I could have been so dense not to see it before. The entire Bible from start to finish is the story of God trying to be in a relationship with us, and trying to teach us how to take that love and grow it in community with each other. Jesus sums it up best when he is asked what the greatest commandment is. He answers, "Love the Lord your God with all your heart, and with all your soul, and with all your mind, and with all your strength. The second is this, 'You shall love your neighbor as yourself.' There is no other commandment greater than these" (Mark 12:30–31).

Love of God, neighbor, and self is at the center of what God is trying to say to us, and has been trying to say since those commandments were first written down in the Old Testament books of Deuteronomy and Leviticus. Jesus didn't dream them up as a new idea to replace the Law of Moses. Jesus was making the point that God's message to human beings hadn't changed. Love God, love each other with a healthy sense of self-love, and you've got it. The whole human project revolves around relationships. Learning how to be in right relationship to God and to each other is the main task of human life.

About the time this was sinking into my brain, I began to notice some patterns in the issues that people in the congregation came to talk with me about. One week in particular was striking. A woman in her forties—let's call her Carol—came in to see me. She had been attending a class I was teaching and she was troubled. One of the questions in a homework assignment asked that she record a time when she really felt the love of God. She couldn't think of one, and that upset her enough to come and talk to me about it.

"I just don't feel that God loves me," she began. "It's like I'm on the outside looking in." We spent the next hour or so going over all the usual ways to connect more closely to God: spending more time in prayer, Bible reading, music, worship. We talked about the difficulties in doing those things and different tips and techniques. She seemed appreciative, but it didn't seem like we were really getting anywhere.

It came time to close our meeting and just as an afterthought I said, "Of course, sometimes the way to come at feeling the love of God is just to practice loving others more." I stood up to open the door for her, but instantly sat back down. Carol had fallen onto the couch sobbing. "That's it!" she wailed. "I've done it to myself! Ever since my divorce, I've been afraid to love anyone else. The wall I built up to keep everyone else out has kept God out, too." For several minutes she sat there and cried. Then she looked up. She smiled. She beamed. She jumped up off the couch like a schoolgirl. "I can't believe it!" she kept saying. "I feel wonderful!" After thanking me a few dozen times, she bounced out of my office and out to her car.

What had just happened? All my profound suggestions of the first hour hadn't made the first bit of difference, and just one little remark that I almost didn't say at all broke through years of pain for her. What was that all about? It seemed that Carol's relationships with others, especially the broken relationship of her marriage, had blocked her relationship with God. How exactly were those things connected? Could human relationships be mirrors of our relationship with the Divine? Well, Matthew 25:31–46 seems to think so, when Jesus says that whatever we do to "the least of these" we have done to him. I knew that, but I was coming to learn it in a different way.

Two days later I met with another class participant named Will. "Others seem to have this sense of God as a loving parent caring for them," he began, "but I've never had that. I just don't feel like God's child."

My musings over the past two days were fresh in my mind, but I still went into my usual routine. I talked a bit about the ways we can use the spiritual disciplines to get closer to God and described the way that closeness can grow over time and practice. It wasn't getting very far. So I changed tracks. "Tell me about your parents," I said.

His mother had died, but it was his father who instantly absorbed his focus. The father was in a nursing home several hours away and the relationship was toxic. As Will was growing up, his father had been a harsh tyrant, demanding that Will follow impossible rules and enforcing them without mercy. Even now that his father was coming close to the end of his life, and Will was going out of his way to try to please him and take care of him, his efforts were met with harsh words or cold stares. Just the previous week, Will had fired off a letter to his father that asked, "Am I your child or not?" I heard that question and my jaw dropped. There it was again. Will didn't have the extreme emotional response that Carol had, but in both cases the root issue was the same. A human relationship had become the stumbling block to a loving relationship with God.

I wasn't trained to help Will work out his relationship with his father, but I could help him see that the problems with his father were being transferred to God. Without realizing it, he'd come to assume that if

God was like a parent then God was like his father. Separating the two began Will's spiritual healing.

After those two back-to-back experiences, I began to think back to other situations. There was Marcie and Walter having marriage trouble. Her complaint? He's too strict with the kids. His complaint? She lets them get away with murder. In Bible studies, both of them had issues with the nature of God. Her issue? God's wrath and judgment. His issue? God's mercy and forgiveness. The issues they could not accept in each other were the same issues they could not accept in God.

I thought about 1 John 4:20: "Those who say, 'I love God,' and hate their brothers or sisters, are liars; for those who do not love a brother or sister whom they have seen, cannot love God whom they have not seen." I felt like I'd stumbled onto the keys of the kingdom. Human relationships are the means by which we find our way to relationship with God. God came in Jesus because we needed God "with skin on." We are finite, limited creatures and need God in the flesh to grasp God's message.

Through the power of the Holy Spirit, we learn to love our neighbor by loving ourselves and we learn to love God by loving our neighbor. Every type of relationship I have has been given to help me grow in the love of God . . . even the difficult relationship with my enemies. Each relationship has its own challenges and gifts that bear fruit spiritually in my relationship with God.

With that idea firmly under my belt, I asked the next question. What then, is the special gift that the marriage relationship offers? In what way does that covenant help us in our relationship with God? Isaiah 54 filled my mind like a warm bath. I remember so well the day I sat in my bed, mourning the losses of my life. My husband had cast me aside, not only for another woman, but for another woman who could give him children, as I could not.

Unable to find rest, I had turned to my Bible and fell to Isaiah 54:1:

Sing, O barren one who did not bear; burst into song and shout, you who have not been in labor! For the children of the desolate woman will be more than the children of her that is married, says the Lord.

I got down to verses 4–6:

Do not fear, for you will not be ashamed; do not be discouraged, for you will not suffer disgrace; for you will forget the shame of your youth, and the disgrace of your widowhood you will remember no more. For your Maker is your husband, the Lord of hosts is his name; the Holy One of Israel is your Redeemer, the God of the whole earth he is called. For the Lord has called you like a wife forsaken and grieved in spirit, like the wife of a man's youth when she is cast off, says your God.

And then down in verse 10:

For the mountains may depart and the hills be removed, but my steadfast love shall not depart from you, and my covenant of peace shall not be removed, says the Lord, who has compassion on you.

It became so clear. The marriage relationship was ultimately about our faithfulness to God. You wouldn't think that would come as such a revolutionary idea to someone who's been in church all her life and read the Bible cover to cover many times. You can't go through either the Old or the New Testament without running into the concept of God's people as God's spouse. The Old Testament is full of God complaining that Israel has been a faithless partner, whoring after other gods and abandoning Yahweh, her first love. The entire book of Hosea is a metaphor for God's faithfulness to Israel in spite of her adulteries. Of course in the New Testament the Church is called the "Bride of Christ," and we don't get very far into early church history before we see her faithlessness.

The very first commandment of the ten given on Sinai—no other gods—is a call to faithfulness—not to many but to one. Perhaps it's the "one" that gives us the most trouble. Think of Jesus' words to Martha as she scurried around the kitchen, mad at Mary who just sat at Jesus' feet in Luke 10:41–42: "Martha, Martha, you are worried and distracted by many things; there is need of only one thing. Mary has chosen the better part, which will not be taken away from her." One thing. One God. Staying faithful to the one is the point.

A covenant relationship to one partner is the gift God gives us so that by learning to be faithful to another person "for better, for worse, for richer, for poorer, in sickness and in health as long as we both shall live" we might eventually be able to do the same with God. In a sense it's practice, but in another sense it's more than that, since our relationship with God goes on simultaneously. As our commitment to our life's partner is strengthened, so is our ability to keep our commitment to God. If either one starts to fail, we can expect both to suffer.

Marriage and Sexuality

So how does sexuality fit into all of that? After all, I can be faithful to another person without being sexual. While I believe marriage is the most common gift God gives for us to experience faithfulness, it's not the only one, or I'd be hopelessly lost as a single person. If I'm not married, I need to find another avenue to learn that lesson of fidelity—maybe with a parent, a child, a friend, or a cause.

That's one reason those who choose a monastic life consider themselves "married" to God and, to a lesser extent, to the Church. Many even wear a wedding band to signify the relationship. In one way, that's the goal for all of us: to be God's committed partner. But instead of learning how to live that out with one person for life, the monastics promise to live it out with one institution for life. Their commitment to the Church becomes the human face that others have in marriage. Both of them have the goal of being the covenant spouse of God.

The adultery commandment, however, has to do very specifically with the sexual part of the marriage covenant. In the time Moses recorded that commandment, and at least down to Jesus' time, it wasn't equally fair to men and women. Monogamy, after all, isn't the rule everywhere, even today, and it was less so back then. Many of the laws of Moses provided that the only woman a man could *not* have was someone already married to another man. He couldn't just sleep with a woman and throw her out—he had to marry her to be considered honorable—but it didn't matter that she was wife number twelve. King Solomon had a thousand wives and concubines. The adultery commandment didn't curb a whole lot of male sexuality.

For the woman, however, there were no multiple marriages in Israelite society. Too bad if she was wife number 146—she couldn't have another husband or be sexual with another man without being called an adulteress and accepting the death penalty that title bore. This commandment put slight limitations on male sexual expression. For many women, it meant celibacy, once the wedding night was over.

Even in Jesus' day, adultery was more tolerated in men than in women. Consider the story of the woman taken in adultery in John 8. We've talked about that story in light of capital punishment, but as we consider the commandment against adultery, let's ask this important question: Where's the man? Those who bring the woman before Jesus are very specific. They caught her in the very act of adultery. The Law of

Moses condemned to death not just the woman, but the man as well. Last I checked, you can't commit adultery by yourself. So where's the guy? Could he have been one of the men who accused her?

But those issues don't excuse adultery, or diminish the need for a commandment forbidding it. In fact, Jesus makes it even more complicated: the sin, he says, starts well before you ever climb into bed with someone. Like all sin, it begins in the heart—"everyone who looks at a woman with lust has already committed adultery with her in his heart" (Matt 5:28). Keeping the commandment is a complicated business.

But why does a commandment about adultery exist at all? Some animals are monogamous and others aren't, yet God doesn't seem to prefer the monogamous Canada goose over the promiscuous bull elk. Since God doesn't give us commandments just for the fun of seeing if we can obey them, there must be something in this odd gift of sexuality that is compromised if human beings use it outside of a committed relationship.

For too long the theology of sexuality that's made its way to church pews has insisted that the gift of sexuality is for the sole purpose of procreation. Well, I can't bear children. Since Paul says that marriage partners are not to deny each other sexually except for a short time by mutual agreement, if sex is only for procreation, then I'm effectively cut out of marriage entirely. But I think that is faulty logic. Human beings don't go into heat like many animals. We have a sexual nature that kicks in regardless of fertility. There's far more to sexuality than reproduction.

So, what's it for? Why did God seemingly give us the promiscuous instincts of the bull elk and the commandment to monogamy of the Canada goose? Like relationships in general, the sexual relationship is meant to help us grow in our relationship to God.

Sexuality is the greatest form of intimacy. After all, the Hebrew word for "naked" also means "vulnerable." In sex, we're vulnerable to another human being—the protective covering of clothing is gone and all the devices we use to make us appear more attractive vanish. In sex, we are what we are and we make that available to another person. When we do that, Genesis says that the "two become one flesh." We are bodily joined and for an instant we are one organism.

That unity is frequently symbolized in a baby—one new life that emerges from two people. The two have become one in this child. But even without the visible reminder of that unity in a child, the miracle still occurs. When a person comes to me wanting to know if it's okay to be sexual with someone, my first question is, "Do you want to be joined to that person for the rest of your life?" I'm not talking about marriage. I'm saying that when you have sexual intercourse with another person, you become one with that person. Whether they become your spouse or whether you never see them again is immaterial. You are forever joined. That's what Scripture claims, and that's what my experience has borne out.

That's the purpose of the gift. Through our sexuality, we can experience in the physical world the spiritual union we're meant to have with God. I see sex doing the same thing for a couple's relationship that the Lord's Supper does for our relationship with God. It makes us one. Our sexuality shows us how deep and all-encompassing is the love of God for us. We don't have to pretend with God. We can be open and vulnerable. We can be naked and helpless and God will still love us. And God won't take advantage of our vulnerability. In Jesus we see that God will become an equally vulnerable partner, offering love always, forcing love never. Sex, to me, is a sacrament, an act that embodies the presence of God or, as the liturgy puts it, "an outward and visible sign of an inward and spiritual grace."

Sexual expression is healthy and helpful only in the context of a covenant relationship where we are committed to being faithful for the rest of our lives. The safety of that covenant lets us be truly vulnerable, and the promise of the permanence of that relationship lets us join ourselves to another. Sex belongs in a permanent, loving, covenant relationship because that's the only place where it's safe.

When we use our sexuality for other purposes—to gain power over others, to run away from our problems, to express our self-loathing— we thwart more than just ourselves. We harm our ability to relate to God, and we give others a false sense that human sexuality is nothing more than an instinct to be satisfied as we please, much as we might decide to eat one, three, or five meals a day. I believe it is more.

Divorce

I'd just finished leading a worship service with a sermon titled "Why Bother Getting Married?" when a noticeably upset older couple came up to see me. He'd been married once before, he said, but that marriage had ended when he came back from World War II. Soon after, he had met this woman who had quickly become the love of his life. They had just celebrated their fiftieth wedding anniversary.

They were contemplating getting a divorce, he said. Oh, they were still very much in love and very happy together after all these years. But in their Sunday School class they had read Jesus' words in Matthew 19:3–9:

> Some Pharisees came to him, and to test him they asked, "Is it lawful for a man to divorce his wife for any cause?"
>
> He answered, "Have you not read that the one who made them at the beginning 'made them male and female', and said, 'For this reason a man shall leave his father and mother and be joined to his wife, and the two shall become one flesh?' So they are no longer two, but one flesh. Therefore what God has joined together, let no one separate."
>
> They said to him, "Why then did Moses command us to give a certificate of dismissal and to divorce her?"
>
> He said to them, "It was because you were so hard-hearted that Moses allowed you to divorce your wives, but from the beginning it was not so. And I say to you, whoever divorces his wife, except for unchastity, and marries another commits adultery."
>
> His disciples said to him, "If such is the case of a man with his wife, it is better not to marry."
>
> But he said to them, "Not everyone can accept this teaching, but only those to whom it is given. For there are eunuchs that have been so from birth, and there are eunuchs who have been made eunuchs by others, and there are eunuchs who have made themselves eunuchs for the sake of the kingdom of heaven. Let anyone accept this who can."

What they heard in those verses was that marrying a second time is adultery. They'd come to the service to find out more, and came to me worried that God couldn't bless the marriage that had given them so much joy for more than fifty years. They believed that God might require them to separate in order to call themselves good Christians. I could hardly speak.

I'm no stranger to this passage and others like it. With two unsuccessful marriages on the books, I know both what it's like to be left and what it's like to do the leaving. I know also that God wasn't particularly pleased with either occasion. Since then, I've also met with many individuals and couples struggling with divorce in one way or another. Sometimes there are issues from a past divorce, and sometimes a marriage is about to break up. One man, separated for ten years from his wife, who lived in another state, hadn't seen or communicated with her in all that time. "I just don't think God wants people to get divorced," he said.

Well, I think he's right. I don't think God likes divorce a single bit. Because I believe marriage is one of the primary ways we learn faithfulness, and because the sexual union in marriage teaches us about becoming one with God and with each other, having that break apart is much worse then never having had the marriage in the first place. When a spouse dies the grief is overwhelming, but the spiritual benefit of learning to be faithful is not undone. In divorce, however, trust is shattered and safety is taken, leading people to question whether they're good enough to be loved for who they are and making it harder to realize that God loves them. As Carol found, it becomes easy to shut love out of our lives for fear of being named unworthy again.

God designed marriage to be for life, so every single divorce is a violation of God's will. It does us spiritual as well as emotional harm, whether we are the divorcer or the divorcee.

But this passage also shows that God doesn't speak in a vacuum. With Moses and the Israelites, God saw when the larger cause of love and justice called for a certificate of divorce to be issued. It was still a rotten business, but sometimes the divorce was less rotten than the alternative. I see this all the time, and there have been occasions when I've advised a couple to fish or cut bait.

For instance, for the couple who hadn't spoken in ten years, the husband's concern over getting a divorce was just a legalism—but Christian marriage isn't a legal entity. It's something that happens in the heart well before a couple walks to the altar, whether they've slept together or not. Sexual intimacy consummates the marriage, but doesn't create it, and a legal document doesn't create a marriage in any religious sense.

I told this man that he was already divorced. In the day that covenant was broken between himself and his wife and they went their separate ways, they had done what God didn't want. They were divorced back then. It's not a piece of paper that creates a divorce; it's the breaking of the relationship. God is pretty neutral about legal documents. It's the relationship that matters.

I've also spoken with people in abusive relationships that are no longer marriages in God's eyes, no matter the law. The covenant of trust, love, safety, and freedom has been broken and the spiritual purpose of marriage undermined. Whether the abuse can be stopped and the trust regained is a matter for those who are trained to help with such issues.

But when people ask me the question from a spiritual angle, the answer is that the thing that God hates has already been done—no additional disfavor is heaped on us just for bringing our legal status into alignment with our spiritual condition.

Some couples masquerade as husband and wife when the marriage is only a shell. Just as going to church doesn't make us Christians, even if we have a baptismal certificate; living in the same house doesn't make us married, even if we have certified copies of the marriage license. Even without overt abuse or other severe problems, this is spiritually damaging. Though the legal marriage may not come to an end, we're morally required to do all in our power to make it authentic.

To begin with, living in a sham of a marriage is dishonest. It teaches children that marriage—one of the primary metaphors for the relationship between God and God's people—is loveless drudgery. It sets the children up for failed relationships with others and a difficult relationship with God. Taking the calling of marriage seriously and doing all in your power to save it and bring it to life provides an excellent example of what Christian life is like. A real marriage is hard work, and so is mature faith. Both require time together, honest communication, repentance, and forgiveness. To couples who are miserably drifting, I issue the challenge: fish or cut bait. Doing nothing isn't neutral—it's harmful.

Though God sometimes allows for divorce, it should never be the first choice, just deciding you're not happy and walking away isn't the Christian way. That's part of Jesus' message in Matthew 19, when he says you shouldn't just get divorced for any reason and, in fact, there are hardly any good reasons for divorce. The disciples—the founders of the Church—balk. Their response? "Hey, if we really have to stick it out, it's better never to get married in the first place." The attitude of even the most faithful was pretty flippant. If they couldn't just dump one wife and get a new one when it suited them, what was the point?

Jesus speaks hard words to a people whose attitudes toward marriage had gone far astray. Maybe I'm wrong, but I don't think Jesus would have spoken that way to the couple who came to me after that service. I'm sure God wasn't happy with the initial divorce, but I'm equally sure that God is delighted that those two found each other and finally were able to learn about real love and faithfulness.

God may have been angry when Israel went running off after other gods. But the story of the relationship between God and Israel is the story of second chances. Anger and disappointment are followed by grace and forgiveness and the chance to start all over again. I don't think God behaves any differently when we mess up. The life of a couple who commit themselves to a lifetime with each other is filled with both joy and difficulty. Marriage is designed by God and given to us so that we might grow in our ability to be faithful, intimate, and loving. When we enter into it, we become one with our partner. When we leave it, it tears a hole in our soul the size of Nevada. God never wants that for us, except as a last-ditch option when all else has failed.

But, when it happens . . . God sits and cries with us, working in our lives to help us understand and learn from our mistakes and leading us to other opportunities to learn how to be faithful. Maybe, as it was for that older couple, it's a new marriage. Maybe it's a path of celibacy or commitment to a cause. There may not be the same chance, but there is another chance . . . another way. The lesson of faithfulness is too important to leave unlearned.

Homosexuality and Same-Sex Marriage

Because I think our human relationships teach us how to be in relationship to God, and because I think marriage is the particular relationship that teaches us about faithfulness, I don't think the gender of the participants is all that important. I'd be happy if my denomination changed its policies and allowed me to conduct weddings for same-sex couples. We're not so overrun with love and faithfulness in this world that we should start trying to put a halt to some expressions of it. When we've eliminated all hatred and violence, then we can come back and see if any of our loves are disordered, but we might find at least as many—maybe more—disordered heterosexual loves as homosexual ones. The caveats about the abuse of sexuality in the previous sections apply across the board.

I know all those Bible verses. I know the ancient Hebrews felt homosexuality was wrong, and I know Paul was against it, too. I also happen to know that those aren't the only verses in Scripture, and I believe that other verses can lead to other conclusions.

I was first faced with this dilemma when I was assigned to my first church in an ultra-conservative area in northwest Florida where neither the congregation nor the town received the arrival of a divorced Yankee woman preacher with aplomb. I was told in no uncertain terms that I was out of the will of God, because Paul said women shouldn't have authority over men and shouldn't speak in church. One day a girl in my youth group said, "My mother says you're evil . . . why?"

I'd been forewarned that getting into the ecumenical clergy group in the town would be tough because of my gender and the conservative nature of the other churches in town. So I was unprepared to be embraced by the president of the Ministerial Association, who pastored an Assemblies of God church, a denomination that allowed for women clergy.

After I had been there a while and had experienced his grace and acceptance, I got up the nerve to ask him about it. "I spent time as a teenager in an Assemblies of God church," I began. "I know that you take Scripture literally. Knowing what the Bible says about women speaking in church and having authority over men, how can you support women pastors?"

His answer was enlightening. "The Bible also says in Galatians 3:28 that in Christ there is no male or female, and Paul clearly used women in positions of authority. The passages are in conflict, but it seems to us that the Galatians passage is meant more universally than the specific problems that Paul mentions with women elsewhere. So we go with Galatians."

That conversation was so refreshing. Here was someone who took Scripture literally, but recognized that not all verses of Scripture were spoken as eternal truths for all time. They were all literal to him, but there were some that were relevant only to a particular time and culture, while others were more universal truths. I had become so tired of women quoting 1 Timothy 2:11–12 at me to show that I couldn't be called to ministry, when they were wearing jewelry, expensive clothes, and fancy hairstyles—all practices that were forbidden just two verses before!

The same applies in the homosexuality debate. People who see no point in following the food laws, who combine cotton and linen fabrics with no moral twinge, and who dismiss killing a child for talking back to her parents as barbaric will pull out the laws about homosexuality as a rule to be enforced.

But consider the sample principle that my Assemblies colleague used. The passages that speak against it are miniscule compared to other sins discussed, and Jesus doesn't mention it once. And there are passages that I see as supportive. The Galatians 3:28 passage is there. When we are in Christ, gender prejudices vanish, along with those of race and class.

Remember the whole verse? "There is neither Jew nor Greek, slave nor free, male nor female, for you are all one in Christ Jesus."

The strongest passages, however, come in the book of Acts as the early church deals with the question of whether Gentiles can become Christians without first becoming Jews by being circumcised and following Jewish law. It begins with God's admonition to Peter in a vision in Acts 10. Remember the sheet that Peter sees coming down? It's filled with unclean animals of every sort—all the stuff forbidden by Scripture. "Eat it," says God. Peter thinks God is testing him and steadfastly refuses, reminding God that it has been forbidden. But the test is different than Peter imagines. God is not testing Peter's faithfulness to Scripture but his obedience to God's commands.

Three times God reminds him that if God has said it is clean, then Peter should eat it without question. No matter that God said something different yesterday. God is alive, not dead. God speaks according to the day and the task and the circumstance. "What God has made clean you must not call profane" (Acts 10:15).

This vision prepares Peter for God's new direction for the church. The Scriptures clearly said that Gentiles were not God's people. They were so unclean that a Jew couldn't enter their homes. Moreover, God had been clear that circumcision was the sign of the covenant—there was nothing else close to it in importance.

But God had been active in the world since the time of Abraham and Moses and continued to be alive and active in the early days of the church. A new time had come. One of the most radical chapters in the Bible is Acts 15. Peter and Paul and James and all the early leaders of the Jewish sect called "The Way" gather to decide how to respond to God's reckless behavior—blessing people who were clearly condemned in the Law of Moses fifteen hundred years before. The gathering at the Council of Jerusalem had to decide who their God was—God or Moses. Were they to obey the words spoken by God long ago or the contrary word God seemed to be speaking now?

In a revolutionary act, these early disciples decided that it was a far greater danger to oppose what God was clearly doing than to abandon what God seemed to want fifteen hundred years earlier. There at the Council of Jerusalem they listened to the experiences of Peter and Paul and Barnabas, who saw the Holy Spirit poured out on those whom Scripture had condemned. Their experiences won the day: Gentile Christians were excused from the requirement of circumcision. They did not have to become Jews. The decision of the Council of Jerusalem was radical—it would be like our contemporary church saying baptism isn't necessary.

It's true that one of the few laws that they did retain for all Christians was the command against "fornication" (which isn't defined), but they also kept in the law against food that still has blood in it. So if you cite Acts 15 as a ban on homosexuality, you also have to go after those who serve rare steaks (and Christians who consume them).

The point of Acts 15, for me, is the same point Jesus makes in Matthew 7:16: "You will know them by their fruits." What is the fruit of the spirit? "Love, joy, peace, patience, kindness, generosity, faithfulness, gentleness, and self-control" (Gal 5:22–23). Human sexuality in both its gay and straight forms has an untold number of perversions. There are many, both gay and straight, who take the name of love and attach it to violence and debasement, humiliation and promiscuity. There are also sexual expressions in both gay and straight forms that represent the highest forms of love, commitment, joy, and fidelity. Better to identify people by their fruit, not by their sexual orientation.

Better too to avoid scapegoating. Sexual sin isn't determined by the gender of the participants. But, even if it were, it's certainly not the greatest sin in the Bible—not even close. Jesus was more concerned with the sins associated with money and possessions and talked about that more than anything else except the Kingdom of God. If there is a sin destroying our nation, I believe it's greed, not homosexuality. But if we focus on same-sex couples, we won't have to look at ourselves and our lifestyles and acknowledge that we might be complicit in the sins of our culture.

Jesus said love was the most important commandment. He said to go into all the world and make disciples, not to go seek out sin and condemn it. However, if you insist that all passages of Scripture are true for all time and in all places, and if you feel your specific calling is to hunt down and eradicate sin, then I invite you to take those sins in biblical order. Do some study and rank the biblical sins according to the number of times they're mentioned. You'll find idolatry at the top, with sins related to money and possessions running a close second. Refusing to care for the poor, ignoring the needs of widows and orphans, cruelty and violence will fill up the top slots in a variety of ways. Homosexuality will be way down on the list.

The focus on homosexuality is also taking the church away from its true mission. On both the liberal and conservative sides, churches have made this agenda their primary focus. But go back to the commandments and consider this: Do not take the name of the Lord your God in vain. No issue, however important, should be the center of the Church. Jesus Christ is the center of the Church.

As Christians we must speak out about injustice and about the ways Christian teaching intersects with daily life and behavior. But important issues can sneak their way into the center, becoming our God—the thing we serve, the reason we exist. The center of the Church is Jesus, and the mission of the Church is to make disciples. Period. Honest devotion to a cause—any cause—can drift into idolatry.

Gender Switching—The Transgendered and Transvestite

These issues aren't new. While it took modern surgical techniques to make it possible for the father of a friend of mine to become her Aunt Mabel, there have always been those who, for one reason or another, haven't felt at home in their gender. I'm not talking about ignoring your feminine or masculine sides. I'm talking about really feeling that the body you were born in is the wrong one. In some cases there are physical abnormalities, where any doctor can tell you at birth you'll have gender issues later on. In other cases the issues are more internal, hormonal, genetic, or have other causes not obvious to the naked eye.

Our society doesn't dole out condemnation equally. The tomboy doesn't suffer the disdain given to a boy who puts on his sister's dress and makeup. It's fashionable for a woman to go to the Oscars in a man's clothing—just check out the red carpet. But a man in drag doesn't get praised for his fashion, except on the rare occasion when it's turned into a freak show or a hit movie. That's a double standard.

But as in other areas of sexuality, the same general rules apply. The purpose of our sexuality is to help us learn to be intimate with God, to be vulnerable and open and given over completely to another. The purpose of marriage is to provide a safe place for that to happen—a relationship where we learn to be faithful to just one, so that we can eventually be faithful to just one God. Within the security of that faithfulness, we can be vulnerable in our sexuality. None of that is gender-dependent. Whether partners are of different genders, same genders, or genders that started out one way and ended up another, they can still achieve the goal.

Sure, some of it is sick. But the root of all sexual sickness is the same. It happens when we abandon God's purpose for marriage and sexuality, and can no longer distinguish sickness from health. If we quit condemning sexual expressions we don't understand and concentrate on issues of love and faithfulness, much of the sickness would be cured— or at least more easily identified.

Think what we could do if we turned our energies from gender to faithfulness. Imagine a constitutional amendment to ban infidelity— not just adultery, but also being unfaithful to parents or children or even pets. If you could eliminate just one thing—gay couples or infidelity— which do you think would make the world a better place? Which would help us come closer to God?

Sexual Abuse

To incorporate violence or coercion into sexual behavior or to make the sexual act humiliating, painful, or anything other than the free and sacred choice of both partners is similar to the violation of the Lord's Supper that was happening in Corinth (1 Cor 12:17–34). In that passage, those who came together for the meal didn't wait for each other. There were distinctions between rich and poor and there was drunkenness and lack of care for what they were doing. The act that was supposed to make all of them one with one another and with Christ was being used with disrespect and caused divisions—just the opposite of what the meal was for. Paul used some of his strongest language in condemning it.

Sexual crimes are the secular form of the same abuse. The abuser creates blocks to our ability to know our unity with God, just as Carol and Will from the beginning of this chapter found that their human relationship issues had created blocks to their relationship with God. While that certainly includes the crimes of rape and other forms of privatized sexual abuse, I want to focus here on the types of sexual abuse that have graduated to billion-dollar industries.

Pornography

Sexuality wasn't given to us as a form of entertainment. It is sacramental in that it helps us become one with God. That's not what happens in the world of pornography. But what exactly do we mean by pornography?

I heard a wonderful story about an African missionary family whose home church was offended that this couple and their children spent all their time with women who wore neither bra nor shirt. They recognized the poverty of the area, however, so the church had a drive to collect T-shirts for all the women so that they could be properly covered. The T-shirts arrived at their destination, and the women were thrilled to get them. They then took the shirts home and promptly cut two round holes in the front of each one of them, so that their breasts would still be available for their God-given function. Decency is often in the eye of the beholder.

Is it pornography when a married couple takes a video of themselves having sex and then watches it together? Some will say yes, others no. We have differing sensibilities, both as individuals and as cultures. But while the debate rages about the decency of Janet Jackson's famous "wardrobe malfunction," the dark underside of the pornography industry goes generally unchecked in Christian churches.

And it is dark indeed. I'm not talking about *Playboy* or even *Debbie Does Dallas*. I'm talking about the violent, sadistic portrayals of both adults and children, where often the photo or video is itself documenting a sex crime. On February 26, 2004, Larry Michael Jeffs was arrested at his California home. Agents seized a video showing Jeffs engaged in sexual acts with a two-month-old girl. Mr. Jeffs videotaped himself molesting the infant and then published it on the Internet.[1] We've got to move our energies from who bears a breast in public and who says a four-letter word on the radio to those who produce and participate in the images that most blatantly encourage sex crimes.

If you doubt the connection between pornography and rape, prostitution, child molestation, and sex trafficking, check it for yourself. Learn about Operation Predator on the website of U.S. Immigration and Customs Enforcement (ICE), where in 2004 more than 1,200 people were arrested worldwide in a massive child pornography case. Of those arrests, 237 were in the U.S., and that was just service providers, not the customers. Here's what happened as they began tracking down subscribers: "Some of the subscribers arrested to date include an elementary school teacher, priests, school principals, school coaches, school janitors, camp counselors, campus ministers, pediatricians, circus clowns, Boy Scout leaders, police officers, firefighters, and many others with direct access to children."[2] Would you really rather spend your energy on Howard Stern?

Jesus pointed out the connection between lust and adultery. Well, it isn't just adultery. Pornography inflames lust and lust heads for the nearest object and method of satisfaction—an object and method that is defined by the pornography. The fantastical perfection of the women in skin magazines does its damage, both to the self-esteem of women and the unrealistic expectations of men, but leave Hugh Hefner and his bunnies be for now—there are bigger fish to fry. Coercion, torture, children, violence. And the prevalence of female victims of pornographic violent lust makes it tantamount to "gendercide."

Prostitution

Prostitution is legal in some places in Nevada, and in both legal and illegal forms it is a boon for tourism. That alone ought to be a concern for those who care about the Ten Commandments, since those tourists are not all single folks. Prostitution facilitates adultery. But it goes much deeper. It's estimated that 162,000 homeless youth are victims of commercial sexual exploitation in the U.S. as well as another 57,800 children in homes.[3]

Next time you turn up your nose and judge that Vegas street walker, remember that 1 in 3 persons involved in street-level prostitution in the U.S. convention and tourist cities is under eighteen years of age. When you leave street prostitution and go indoors it is 1 in 2.[4] And it isn't a great leap from prostitution to sex trafficking. Again, don't just take it from me—listen to U.S. State Department statistics.

- Where prostitution is legalized or tolerated, there is a greater demand for human trafficking victims and nearly always an increase in the number of woman and children trafficked into commercial sex slavery.
- Of the estimated 600,000 to 800,000 people trafficked across international borders annually, 80 percent of victims are female, and up to 50 percent are minors. Hundreds of thousands of these women and children are used in prostitution each year.
- A 2003 study published in the *Journal of Trauma Practice* found that 89 percent of women in prostitution want to escape, 70–95 percent were physically assaulted, and 68 percent met the criteria for post traumatic stress disorder in the same range as treatment-seeking combat veterans.[5]

Sex Trafficking

Finally, the road reaches its inevitable destination: human trafficking. The trafficking industry provides organized crime with annual profits of about $8–10 billion.[6] Of the 600–800 thousand people trafficked across borders each year, 14,500–17,500 are coming into the United States, and in all regions, of those who are trafficked, 33 percent of women, 23 percent of girls, 10 percent of boys, and 1 percent of men are sold for forced or coerced commercial sex.[7]

All of that has a lot to do with a whole lot of commandments, but I didn't just include it here because pornography, prostitution, and sex trafficking help to push some otherwise faithful people over the adulterous edge. I put it here because at the heart of the adultery commandment is the foundation of both the Jewish and Christian understanding of God—that God can be "known." We are invited to intimate relationship with God, and the image of God as faithful, loving, and intimate spouse is far more prevalent in Scripture than even the image of God as Father.

When sex is cruel or trivialized, we've harmed the ability of others to enter into loving relationship with God. In a sense, we've damned them—not because God won't welcome them, but because they'll believe themselves unworthy of welcome and will stay away. We understand the love of God through loving relationship with others. We understand that it is safe to be completely open and vulnerable with a faithful God by experiencing that safety in sexual union with a covenant partner. Sexual abuse damages our ability to know God's love.

There are things we can do, if we have the will. We can quit yelling about shock jocks on the radio and begin to pay attention to the people being sold into sexual slavery in our own country. We can stop looking down our noses at the prostitutes and lobby for the prosecution of the pimps. And somebody needs to pick up the rock of the convention and tourism industry and expose the places where it turns a blind eye to prostitution and trafficking.

■○■○■

"Thou shalt not commit adultery": The issue is faithfulness to our most intimate partners so we can learn about being faithful to the one who is nearer to us than our breathing. We fail early and often in that, but our faithful God offers again to take us back, encouraging us like the adulteress in John 8 to "Go and sin no more."

As the Bride of Christ, we need to find our common ground. In the issues of life and death, we can at least agree that our desire is to preserve life and mourn death, even though we may disagree on how to achieve that goal. Here, let's agree that our sexuality is a sacred gift, and that God's concern with fidelity is far broader than biblical concerns about the correct partner.

If we can learn to be faithful—to our spouses, to our children, to the principles of freedom and justice that give us our humanity—we can tackle the other questions.

Whose Is It, Anyway?

Thou shalt not steal.

The definition of stealing is easy: taking for yourself something that belongs to another. But it doesn't take long before we get into the nuances. Is stealing ever justified? What about the woman who steals bread to feed her family or the man who steals back the pocket watch that was first stolen from his grandfather? What about the biological parent who kidnaps his child? What about atoning for the theft of land from Native Americans or Scottish Highlanders?

The issue is more complicated than it seems at first. And the first place to begin to untangle it is by looking at ownership, something the Bible is very clear about: "The earth is the Lord's and all that is in it, the world, and those who live in it" (Ps 24:1). The people of God are to see themselves as stewards, not owners, of all that is.

The vexing part is that this is *not* the American way. As an exercise at stewardship workshops, I often ask participants to share with each other what their life was like in a particular fifteen-year span. The catch is, they are to do it without using the possessive pronouns "My/mine" or "Our/ours." Instead they are to substitute a reference to the true owner by saying either "God's" or "the x that God gave me." The exercise is not without its pitfalls. Talk of "God's wife" is pretty unsettling; and in some difficult cases, "The parents that God gave me" makes God complicit in some real atrocities. Nevertheless, it does help us see just how often we stamp things that clearly cannot be owned with the grasping label "mine."

On a national scale, this is overwhelming. I am dumbfounded when I hear talk of owning part of the ocean or, even worse, "our airspace." Our airspace? How can we possibly think it is possible to own the air? And what exactly is that American flag doing on the moon? We take land ownership for granted, but it was not always so. The reason we were able to swindle Native Americans out of Manhattan for $24 worth of beads is that their culture was too spiritually sophisticated to think that land could be bought or sold. They knew perfectly well that human beings could not own the earth. It was given for us to use and protect by the Great Spirit, who owned it all. It never occurred to them they were selling land.

Our belief that we can own whatever we please has gotten us into heaps of trouble. Thinking we could own human beings as slaves left a deep wound in the American soul, and it is still destroying both bodies and souls today in Niger and other places around the globe. Our idolization of the owner today means that the rich get richer and the poor get poorer and the former sees no responsibility for the latter.

I once attended a clergy conference at a famous coastal resort. The host organization was feeling generous, knowing that clergy can't usually afford such luxuries, so they housed us in opulent apartments and scheduled meetings in the golf club where a major golf tournament is held.

While we appreciated the benevolence, so many of us were unhappy that we begged the organization never to send us back there again. Why? The accommodations were comfortable, but our souls were not. The racism was palpable—black workers held jobs that shielded them from paying guests. And in a clubhouse adorned with paintings of famous golfers, the only blacks portrayed were golf caddies. Not even Tiger Woods made the cut.

But it wasn't only the racism that made us uncomfortable. Our conference took place in the off-season, which meant that most of the yachts were in the harbor, and most of the homes unoccupied. Yet there were homeless people in that state, plenty of them, while here, hundreds—even thousands—of homes were occupied for just a short time. But of course the homeless could not live there. Those homes and apartments were "owned" by others. Some were third and fourth homes. How many homes does one person need?

A couple of colleagues and I went wandering around the harbor, and we stopped at a small ice cream shack staffed by a black woman. As we told her that we were ministers, her faith came to life and she told of all God had done for her. She was grateful for the tiniest blessings, but as she spoke, the injustice of our surroundings became even more apparent. She lived just a few miles away, in a run-down mobile home with a leaky roof that the landlord wouldn't fix, and though she had a serious illness, she couldn't afford medical care.

If that woman had thrown a rock, it would have gone into the harbor. And there in the harbor were yachts, waiting for the few weeks that their "owners" would come and use them. Selling even one of those boats would have supplied the black woman's whole neighborhood with adequate housing, food, and medical care for a very long time.

She asked us to pray for her, and when we got back to the afternoon session of our conference, we raised her up to our other colleagues. And we asked never to return to that place. The conference organizers surely thought this setting was a beautiful gift, but I couldn't go by the scene without tears in my eyes, rage in my heart, and a prayer for the woman who had daily reminders that she was a nobody in the world of ownership and privilege.

On the one hand it seems like we should be able to have some space that is reserved for us, but is it possible to have too much? Would there be any such thing as private property in a moral universe?

Stealing of Property

Private Property

Any student of the book of Acts can tell you that private property was suspected by the very first Christians. Their mode of living in those fledgling years is described in Acts 2:43–45: "Awe came upon everyone, because many wonders and signs were being done by the apostles. All who believed were together and had all things in common; they would sell their possessions and goods and distribute the proceeds to all, as any had need."

Such communal living seemed to be the norm, at least for a time, but it doesn't appear that it was required of everyone—the way of life described in Acts 2 seems to have been voluntary.

We don't know how many people participated in this time of communal living, but we do know that it represented some of the most basic beliefs of the early Christian community. In *The Early Christians in Their Own Words*, Eberhard Arnold writes:

> According to Christians, the private ownership of property was the result of sin. However necessary property might be for life in the present demonic epoch, the Christians could not cling to it. The private larder or storeroom had to be put at the disposal of guests and wanderers just as much as the common treasury.[1]

Why was private ownership a spiritual problem? That's as easy to see today as then. When some are allowed to fence off some of God's resources with no outside check on whether they have more than they need, greed will take over and some will go without. Those who choose to follow Jesus are to take a different path. Reminded that "Foxes have holes, and birds of the air have nests; but the Son of Man has nowhere to lay his head" (Matt 8:20), Christian disciples were to use their God-given resources to help others. Arnold goes on to describe the giving of the early church:

> Even in the smallest church community, the overseer had to be a friend of the poor, and there was at least one widow responsible to see to it, day and night, that no sick or needy person was neglected. The deacon was responsible to find and help the poor and to impress on the rich the need to do their utmost. Deacons also served at table. There was no excuse for anyone because he had not learned or was unable to do this service. Everybody was expected to go, street by street, looking for the poorest dwellings. As a result, Christians spent more money in the streets than the followers of other religions spent in their temples.[2]

The designation "private property" (whether belonging to individuals, corporations, or nations), guarantees poverty, because it restricts access to resources. I don't think it's too much of a stretch, given our human failings, to think it also guarantees murder and war. If we truly had the sense that the property, possessions, and resources that are, by law, under our authority belonged to God, and that it was God who had the ultimate say in who received them, I suspect life would look very different.

Public Space

The protection of both wilderness and public space can help us remember that God's resources are meant for all. Setting aside land that cannot be privately owned is about the only policy left that reminds us of the truth about ourselves and our world. We are not owners. We are stewards. We need to make provision for the poor. We also need to make provision for the earth.

While we looked at the protection of land in the Sabbath chapter, the plight of the city park more properly belongs here. The Trust for Public Land, founded in 1972, was the first national conservation organization with an explicit urban component, created in response to the desperate plight of urban parkland, which had grown worse since World War II.

The benefits of city parks were highlighted by the creation of New York's Central Park in 1859, setting a benchmark for cities across the country. At the height of the city park movement, between 1890 and 1940, life in the city was highly desirable. But after the war came the move to the suburbs, and with it the idea that people with big backyards didn't need public parks. They had their own.

At that moment, we forgot the poor. Those who could afford to own land had much of what parks provided. Those who couldn't buy land or a car to commute to work remained in the cities, where the parks were neglected. Public spaces that once provided gardens, ball fields, and hiking trails; places that taught ecology, hosted concerts, protected wildlife, and mitigated flood waters—those places began to suffer from over or under-use, deteriorating equipment, erosion, weeds, graffiti, and crime.

Only one-third of the children in Los Angeles live within walking distance of a public park or other open space. Only 42 percent of the children in Dallas have that privilege, compared to 97 percent of the children in Boston and 91 percent in New York City.[3] If the prophets Micah and Amos lived today, one would be headed to L.A. and the other to Dallas to proclaim in their streets: "Remember the poor!"

The Centers for Disease Control and Prevention reports that "Americans living closer to parks are more likely to exercise regularly, leading to weight loss, increased energy, and better overall health."[4] Because parks filter pollutants from the air and help with storm water drainage, they provide environmental benefits and urban police departments have documented sharp declines in juvenile arrests after recreational facilities opened in low-income neighborhoods.[5]

God's provision has ensured that practicing good stewardship isn't just sacrificial. It's beneficial to our life together in community. It's an act of justice. To allow those with means to scoop up earth and air, sea and sky, and wall it off from the poor is stealing—from God, who owns it, and from the poor, whom God meant to use it. We won't say goodbye to private property anytime soon, so we need to stop and think about what we're doing.

We're not just talking about the city park. What does it mean that people have to pay to get into many of our national parks? Driving into Yellowstone will set you back $20; walking in, $10. God knows they need the funding, and I wouldn't take away a dime of their revenue. But why aren't we funding these amazing resources another way so that they can be truly public space? And amusement park fees usually are either completely out of reach for the poor, or completely unsafe. As of this writing you can enjoy the wonders of Disney World for one day for $59.75 if you are age ten or older or a mere $48.00 for kiddies ages three to nine. And how many three-year-olds go to Disney alone?

And then there's the coastline. Organizations like the Surfrider Foundation, dedicated to the preservation of oceans, waves, and beaches, keep an eye on how much of our coastline is open to the public. Hats off to Hawaii, where Surfrider reports all beaches are publicly owned. Now if I could only afford the plane fare! Lots of people take off on spring break to Florida beaches, where 67 percent of them are privately owned and there is only one access point for every 10,000 residents. Three-quarters of the beaches in Massachusetts are privately owned. By contrast, California has 60 percent of its coastline still open to the public.

The same sort of thing is happening with movies—the cheap Saturday matinees of the past have given way to ticket prices that keep the poor out of theaters entirely. One of the reasons? Home theaters. Just as we figured we could own our own park in the backyard, now we can own a theater in our basement. As of this writing, you can buy a sixty-three-inch plasma TV. The haves are putting these in their homes and buying DVDs, driving up the prices in the theaters, which are already out of reach for most residents of low-income neighborhoods. Like the city parks, bargain theaters suffer from under- or overuse, broken equipment, and poor maintenance

Many churches that once were public community centers have moved out to the suburbs, making them useless for many ministries to the poor. There's no point in serving free meals for those who have no car to drive to your location. There are still some churches which have remained in the cities and there are certainly some that work to reach out to their neighborhoods, but overall, the neighborhood church is one more loss of public space in the last fifty years.

Private property is probably here to stay, but Christians should be mindful that God is the true owner of both their backyard and their plasma TV. Remembering the eighth commandment, we should be mindful of the ways in which private ownership can steal from the poor, and work for public parks, public beaches, public entertainment, and public squares that are well-funded, equitably placed, and free or afford-able to all.

Affordable Housing

Those who can pay more for housing and those eager to receive more in a sale are gradually taking affordable housing away from even the average American. Here are some numbers.

In my town, 25 homes were sold in September of 2005 at an average price of $487,000, down from the previous month, when 42 homes were sold for an average of $526,000. I live in the greater Boston area, with notoriously high housing prices, but prices nationwide followed the same trends. In 2004, the median price for an existing home was $188,900,[6] meaning half the homes in the U.S. sold for more, and half for less. The median household income was $44,684 (unchanged from 2003),[7] again meaning that half the households made more, half made less.

So I went to one of the online mortgage calculators. If I were buying that lovely median existing home at $188,900 at a fixed 5.4 percent interest over 30 years with no money down, my mortgage payment would be $1,060.73 per month, excluding property tax. That's just over 28 percent of that median income spent on housing costs.

Banks won't lend to me if my monthly mortgage payment is more than 28 percent of my gross monthly income, so I'm right at the upper limit. But banks include property tax in the calculation, and that's not included in the previous figure. That means I may have difficulty getting a loan, unless I can come up with a 20 percent down payment. That down payment would amount to $37,780. If I manage to put away $500 per month, I could save that down payment in just over six years.

Oops . . . I almost forgot. I'm a woman. Scratch all that. The median income for a *woman* in America is only $31,374.[8] But my median will be a bit higher, since I'm white. The median income for a Hispanic woman is $24,030.[9] Looks like we'll both be renting.

But that's not so easy either. Rental prices can be pretty nasty, but the thing that keeps bringing people to the coffers of church discretionary funds is the need to come up with the initial deposit to get into a rental property. When you're living from paycheck to paycheck, there's no way to put that much away into savings. I could apply for government housing, but I can't get my name on a priority list for such housing because I'm living with my brother. To qualify as "homeless" and thus be a top priority for such assistance, I've got to be in a shelter or on the street.

While many cry out for developers to create more affordable housing, the not-in-my-backyard syndrome is still strong. Many neighborhoods resist low-income and subsidized housing—and developers want more money—which means fewer and fewer units affordable to the average worker. But creating affordable housing isn't impossible. It's a matter of the will to follow Amos in his cry: "Let justice roll down like waters, and righteousness like an ever flowing stream" (Amos 5:24).

Congregations can band together to lobby for affordable housing in their towns. The United Methodist church in Exeter, New Hampshire, worked with a local developer to be sure that affordable housing was included in a development abutting their church property. Christian developers have a huge opportunity to put their faith into practice in their business and contribute to the public good. Individual Christians can work to create neighborhoods that welcome affordable housing units. If we must own private property, we have to be sure that the poor have a means of ownership as well. Otherwise we have, again, stolen from the poor.

Tithing and Faith-Based Initiatives

Many Christians tithe, which is the practice of giving 10 percent of one's income to God, the biblical standard for our charitable giving. But most don't, as the state of most church finances will tell you. Christians, though, should consider the words of the prophet Malachi, who accuses those who do not tithe as "robbing God" (Mal 3:8).

There's truth to that. If every Christian gave 10 percent to God, ministry could happen in ways we never dreamed. Churches would no longer need to have pledge drives or make constant pleas for money. Non-profit organizations would have enough to care for all who needed their services. Tithing might even result in lower taxes, since some government programs wouldn't be necessary if the Church and other non-profits had the funds to provide them.

It has been suggested that some church mission projects could be funded not just by a tithe, but through a partnership between the government and faith-based organizations. I'm not entirely comfortable with that idea. I get nervous about Church-state lines getting blurred and about the tendency for bureaucracy and red tape to impede the mission. In general, government involvement means tons of additional forms and administrative oversight. Dealing with that either overtaxes workers or grows the budget, decreasing the percentage of each dollar that goes directly to the work.

In addition, many faith communities are justifiably hesitant about involvement in a program to address a given societal need while being barred from proclaiming why they are doing so. But I do agree with the basic premise that if congregations were truly living out their faith in their communities, we would need fewer federal programs and that care for the less fortunate would be more efficient, better suited to the populations served, and better able both to stem abuse of the system and to adjust to individual circumstances.

Tithing is not a public issue in and of itself, but learning to tithe to charitable organizations is a key to adequate funding for many public missional efforts.

My mother was once part of the national Tithing Task Force for the American Baptist Churches, and I've been tithing since the time I had an allowance. I have given 10 percent when I had a comfortable income, and I gave 10 percent when the only money I had was what people gave to me as charity. When I was in seminary I tithed my scholarship money. You will not find me condemning the practice of tithing.

But I do want to issue a warning. With a focus on tithing, it becomes very easy to assume that 10 percent belongs to God and 90 percent belongs to me. That is not biblical. I tell congregations that if a pastor is just asking you to tithe, then thank your lucky stars and shut up. What the Bible actually teaches is that 100 percent belongs to God. Most of the time, God allows us to use 90 percent for other things, and just asks that we give 10 percent as a good-faith token that we understand whose it really is. But sometimes God requires more than 10 percent. Sometimes God asks that we sell all we have and give to the poor. Sometimes God requires something in between. The real point is that we own none of it. God cares about the 10 percent we give, because that is the sign of our understanding. But God also cares about how we use the other 90 percent, because that other 90 percent belongs to God, too. We only have it in trust.

Tithing also has a corporate dimension. Just as personal morality isn't enough, it's not enough for congregational leadership to push individuals to tithe. The church itself should practice what it preaches. Look at your church budget. Does at least 10 percent go outside of your doors to the larger world? If your church is part of a larger denomination, does at least 10 percent of that larger budget go beyond itself?

Suppose Christian-owned businesses and corporations and not just the individual owners tithed their profit? What if the United States government tithed its budget to Africa? Former Ambassador to South Africa James Joseph asked in 2004,

> Why is the United States so generous domestically and so stingy abroad when borders no longer create or confine community? While the nineties was one of our most prosperous decades ever, our nation also set a record for stinginess abroad. Never has the U.S. given a smaller share of its money to help the world's poor. We now spend less than half of what we spent a decade ago as a proportion of our GDP. The U.S. gives less foreign aid than any of the other industrialized nations, proportionate to the size of its economy. The top five donor countries at the dawn of the new millennium are Denmark, Norway, Netherlands, Sweden, and Luxembourg. The United States is twenty-first.[10]

Can you imagine what could happen around the world if the United States decided to tithe? There are enough resources in the world for everyone, but only if those who control them recognize that we're stewards and not owners of those resources. God has already laid out the basic standard for handling profit: 10 percent, off the top, given away to help the work of God's Kingdom, with more required under special circumstances. "Will you rob God?" asks the prophet Malachi (Mal 3:8). Suppose the United States tithed? What if the President put a commitment to *that* in a State of the Union speech? *That* would be a faith-based initiative.

Stealing of Humanity

It's not only property that we steal. In many ways this commandment is a prelude for the last two on the list, as we steal reputations with our false witness and develop a heart that is willing to steal through our covetousness. But perhaps the most insidious form of stealing is the way we steal the humanity of others by treating them as something other than human, taking their dignity, and declaring ourselves superior. We name the way we do that with "isms": racism, sexism, ageism, classism. The person may become an object or an animal, or may seem to disappear entirely, as we look through them as if they had no independent existence at all. We have stolen their humanity.

Racism

His name was Billy, and in 1966 he moved to my town when we were both in the second grade. He was the only black child in our school and his family the only black family in our town. It was only later that I learned how my parents had gone to town meetings to fight for the right for Billy's family to buy the lovely house up on the hill, or the work they had done to make Billy's family accepted in our American Baptist church. It was only later that I had any understanding of why my father, a high school administrator, was always taking pictures of Billy and me together. He said he was showing them at assemblies at school, but I couldn't figure out why all those high school students would want to see pictures of me and my friends.

I didn't know what was happening in the country at the time, and in my childlike innocence, I didn't know why Billy was different. When boys ganged up on him and beat him up, I thought it was just because he was the new kid. We were friends for years.

At last, different high schools called us in different directions. I learned in history class about slavery and the Civil War. I knew slavery was very wrong. I learned about how we put the Indians on reservations and took away their land, and I knew that was wrong, too. But I thought it was history. In Sunday School we sang, "Red and yellow, black and white, they are precious in his sight. Jesus loves the little children of the world." I thought the sins of the past were over. I was very wrong.

I think the first inkling I had that racism was alive and well was at Thanksgiving. I don't remember how old I was when I first began to understand, but there always seemed to be a lot of arguing at our Thanksgiving dinners. It was a large family affair with often twenty or so gathered at our house. The center of the tension seemed to be my grandfather, a kind man in many ways but who was also the incarnation of Archie Bunker.

The woes of the city where he lived, and indeed the country in general, could all be traced to the "coloreds," who committed crimes and brought down property values and didn't teach their children. Grandpa always felt free to express his opinions, at which point his children would jump on him for being a bigot and the fur would start to fly.

Grandpa's own experiences didn't seem to make any difference to him. He met and worked with many people of color across his ninety-two years, and he liked all of them, but each one was always the exception to the rule. He never could do the math and think that perhaps his rule was flawed.

Because of my experience of my grandfather, I thought that racism was always open and blatant. I thought it meant taking slaves or doing someone physical harm or calling them names. I thought it was pretty much restricted to people who refused to associate with people of another race or who wouldn't eat in the same places or walk on the same side of the street. Of course those are forms of racism, and those forms still exist. I have lived in towns where I have seen it with my own eyes.

A friend who was a real estate agent in Florida sold a house in the "white" part of town to a black woman and got an angry call from the mayor. In that same area, the high school had to move the location of their senior banquet because the restaurant they'd initially chosen was in a neighborhood considered unsafe for the black students after dark. Hate groups are on the rise. When I invited a black woman and her white husband to attend the all-white church I was serving, threatening messages were left on my desk. Even blatant forms of racism are still alive and well in America.

But racism runs so insidiously deep in our country that there are many forms we don't see—like the fact that I've been writing this section using the word "we," when what I mean are white people. People of color see the more subtle forms quite easily and when they raise their voices in protest "we" dismiss their concerns as unimportant or ridiculous.

Certainly there are forms of racism that exist in non-white communities, but I can't talk about those because I'm not a part of it. I can talk about white racism because I am a part of that culture, and because it has ruled America for centuries. Which is part of the point. The more subtle forms of racism today are tied to the reality of "white privilege," the fact that in American culture, white people are given opportunities and privileges others are not. We don't usually know it, because we're not being shut out. We don't notice that things are designed for us because we're not looking for something different.

Take hairstyling, for example. When I arrived at seminary in Atlanta, I had to find a new hairdresser. After a phone-book search, I wound up at a salon focused on styling black people's hair. I was the only white person in the building, and everyone was a bit perplexed about why I was there.

I looked around. There were hair-styling implements that I'd never seen before. They looked a bit dangerous to me. I didn't know what to do. I didn't want to cause offense, but I wasn't sure if I was being more offensive by leaving or by staying. I didn't want to give the impression that I was unwilling to be in a black salon, so I stayed—and got the best conditioning treatment of my life.

But that experience made me realize that the hair of black women is substantially different than the hair of white women. The fact that I'd never seen many of those instruments before made me realize that the salons where I usually went weren't equipped to deal with a black person's hair. How frustrating it must be for black women in predominantly white towns to try to find a place that can style their hair. I'd never really thought about how fortunate I was to be able to walk into any hair salon and find people who know how to deal with my hair. It was a privilege I had that my black friends did not, and I had been completely unaware.

I began to learn other things. How some scholarship applications asked for pictures to be sure the applicant was white. How my black male friends with nice cars were stopped more frequently on the highway by police and how people of color were searched more frequently in airports. How some African Americans have to carry their ATM withdrawal slips with them to prove how they got the money in their wallets. How upsetting it must be to a woman of color to look for makeup in a store and see a pasty-white powder named "natural." How walking into a new place where there are white people is never truly safe.

"But it's not my fault!" I hear white people say, over and over. "I can't be blamed because I get a job and someone else doesn't . . . I don't even know who else applied." "I never owned slaves. I don't owe them anything." Well, maybe not, but look at it this way for a minute.

Let's suppose that my great-great-grandfather was a scoundrel who swindled your great-great-grandfather out of everything he had, reducing your family to abject poverty. He got your ancestor's land, slandered his name so he couldn't get a job, and finally even took his home with all his belongings.

Time and generations passed. Unfortunately, your family has never really been able to dig out of that hole. The children had to go to work young and couldn't go to school, which left them out of the running for good jobs when they got older and consigned them to dangerous positions in factories and mines. So their children, too, had to take on extra responsibilities early. They've lived in a poor section of town and haven't always had the best influences around them. Life for you is still a struggle today.

Life for me, however, is golden. My great-great-grandfather was seen as a shrewd businessman, and his company rewarded him. He left a fortune to his children, who sent my grandparents to the finest schools and provided them with leisure time to make all the right connections for success. I've inherited the family home in the best part of the city, and the house is full of expensive antiques. In fact, I'm writing all this on a lovely old desk that once belonged to your great-great-grandfather. Sorry you're in such a state, but it's not my fault. I didn't do it. I don't see that I owe you anything.

Really? Nothing at all? Not even the desk?

Although some steps have been made, white people still have the lion's share of the power in this country, and we still enjoy the benefits bought at the cost of millions of lives stolen by our great-great grandfathers. White people are not off the hook.

The Bible and Racism

Where do we go in the Bible to think through this issue? Because the Bible was used for so long to support the practice of slavery, it may be hard for some to feel safe looking there. Both Old and New Testaments describe how a master should treat a slave, which slave owners considered biblical justification for the institution of slavery. Surely God would have spoken out against it if it were so wrong, but instead God gave instructions about how to do it.

That attitude represents a fundamental misunderstanding of Scripture. God does not speak in a vacuum. As Christians, we proclaim a personal God interested in particular people at particular places and times, not a distant God who cannot either know or be known. Ours is a God who relates, who works with us where we are and as we are, while trying to move us along the road to salvation. God's instructions for the humane treatment of slaves and for slaves to be above reproach is simply God meeting people where they are and gradually trying to move them toward faithfulness so that they can say with Paul in Galatians

3:28: "There is no longer Jew or Greek, there is no longer slave or free, there is no longer male or female; for all of you are one in Christ Jesus."

A similar progression happens with laws about revenge. God begins with "eye for eye, tooth for tooth" (Deut 19:21), which sounds harsh to our modern ears, but which was a step ahead of other contemporary cultures that were taking a life for an eye, a whole family for a tooth. God's first step is toward the most basic equity, fairness. It's about fifteen hundred more years before the people are ready to hear "turn the other cheek." Moral development occurs across history as well as across a lifetime.

If you really want to see what God thinks of slavery, look at the Exodus. Time and time again, God instructs Israel to treat the stranger and the foreigner with kindness and tolerance by reminding them of the horrors of their own slavery. The clearest message to me in all those accounts is, "Don't do that. Don't become slaveholders at all. Anyone who works for you should have an opportunity to get out, to be free." You see it in law after law, especially those related to Sabbath and Jubilee.

In the New Testament the prominent racial tensions are between the Jews and the Samaritans, and Jesus is clear that he's not in favor of the separation. While other Jews coming from north to south in Palestine went to great lengths (literally) to avoid setting foot in Samaria, Jesus walks straight in. Moreover, he stops, has his disciples buy food there, and has the longest conversation recorded in the Gospels with a Samaritan woman (John 4:1–42). The hero of one of his most famous parables is the "good Samaritan" (Luke 10:25–37), and when Jesus heals ten lepers in Luke 17:16, he notes that it is only the Samaritan who comes back to say thank you.

Another deep suspicion, if not downright animosity, was between Jews and Gentiles, the word for anyone who was not a Jew. Laws of separation forbade Jews from entering Gentile homes or eating with Gentiles, who were not to receive the benefits that the Jews had and were only allowed in the very outer courts of the temple.

Jesus indicates that he is specifically called to the Jews (Matt 15:24) in his three-year ministry, but once that ministry has been broadened through the power of the Holy Spirit in Acts, things are much different. God has some retraining to do, but in Acts 10, Peter finally "gets it" through the vision of the unclean animals in the sheet we looked at earlier. In Acts 15 the church finally votes to end the separation, and the once totally Jewish sect called "The Way" becomes one body in Christ with Gentiles. Both Jesus and the early church refused to discriminate on the basis of race or ethnicity.

Remember my great-great grandfather? The modern idea that present generations bear no responsibility for the sins of the past isn't a biblical understanding. While there are a few passages like Ezekiel 18:20: "The person who sins shall die. A child shall not suffer for the iniquity of a parent, nor a parent suffer for the iniquity of a child: the righteousness of the righteous shall be his own, and the wickedness of the wicked shall be his own," there are plenty of passages that sound more like the language back in the first commandment in Exodus 20:5b–6: "For I the Lord your God am a jealous God, punishing children for the iniquity of parents, to the third and the fourth generation of those who reject me, but showing steadfast love to the thousandth generation of those who love me and keep my commandments."

But beyond the language of reward and punishment, the people of Israel never saw themselves as individuals apart from the history of their people. Time and time again we see Israel looking back at its history, seeing the sins of many generations past and going to great lengths of repentance to atone for them. The Christian doctrine of the Communion of Saints indicates that we are connected to Christians across both time and space. We are one with them. It is also the concept of the global village. What happens to one happens to all.

As I have researched my genealogy, I've read about the Robertson clan in Scotland. The clan crest has a shield with three wolves' heads. No one is sure why the wolf ended up on the Robertson shield, but one speculation is that they were responsible for killing the last wolf in Scotland. Call me crazy, but that cuts through this wolf-lover's heart like a steel blade. I feel driven in at least some small way to atone for the sins of my ancestors by helping with wolf recovery efforts in whatever way I can. I've come to feel connected to my heritage and my ancestors in a way that's hard to explain if you haven't experienced it, and I want to atone for their sins.

Americans feel that connection on some level. On the Fourth of July, we wave flags as if we were the ones who founded our country. When we know that our ancestors founded a school or settled a town, we walk around like we own the place. It only seems to be when our forebears did things that were not so noble that we want no part in their actions and we claim to have no connection and no responsibility. I believe the Bible calls us to repentance, both for our own sins and for the sins of our ancestors. White people, especially, need to be on their knees. Christians need to work hard to abolish racism.

Sexism

When racism has taken hold, we tend to see the "other" as sub-human. In the early days of our country we called them "savages," referring to Africans or Native Americans. The British used the term to refer to the Scottish Highlanders who were all lumped together as some sort of animal species. In the case of sexism, however, the problem is not seeing someone as another species but in seeing the other person as an object.

Of course there are issues with sexism for both women and men. Men do it to women, yes. But women do it to men and to other women, and we even manage to do it to ourselves. Gender issues are difficult ones, even beyond the homosexuality debate. In 2005 Larry Summers, then the president of Harvard University, was trying to swim upstream after suggesting that women just weren't wired in a way that allowed them to excel in science and engineering. Statements like that get a lot of press, but the roots of sexism are more subtle.

Let's begin at the beginning with Adam and Eve. It seems impossible to me that people could blame all the sin and evil in the world on women because of Eve, and yet I've heard it taken seriously and felt its effects. If you want to play Bible prooftexting, then I offer this: In Romans 8:2, Jesus got women off the hook, by setting us free from the law of sin and death. And Galatians 3:28 confirms that in Christ there is no male or female. And besides, Eve wasn't even created when God gave the command. The prohibition was given to Adam.

The beautiful part of the Creation story in Genesis 1–2 is that God created us male and female, which represents the image of God. Every time I teach a class and gather a group of people to really study Scripture, someone reads Genesis 1 and notices that God speaks in the plural in verse 26: "Let us make humankind in our image." Is that evidence for the Trinity? Maybe. But here's another one for the hopper. Maybe it's evidence of God as the unity of two genders, which he images in the next verse in two distinct forms, male and female. Maybe the second creation story in Genesis 2 illustrates this by having Eve taken from Adam's side—out of the one emerge two.

It's worth considering that God might not be a particular gender or without gender but rather fully both genders. That certainly gives a theological basis for recognizing gender differences in a way that honors them equally.

The lack of such honor is the problem in sexism. Scholars such as Carol Gilligan, Deborah Tannen, and others have helped us to realize that women and men have significant internal differences. Decades of women trying to pretend they were the same as men has done some considerable harm, and perhaps the under-representation of women in the science and engineering fields is merely a reflection of male-oriented research methods. Maybe women go about research differently. If the methodology of women were equally understood and honored, we might open up entirely new avenues of research.

Just as many things in American culture were designed by Caucasians and reflect the often unconscious biases of white America, so many of those same things were designed by men and reflect the male way of thinking and behaving. That's not wrong. But it's important to be more conscious of the ways in which the structures, tests, and environments that we design reflect the bias of our own race, gender, and culture so that we can level the playing field for everyone.

We have to quit viewing people as objects. Pornography does this, and not only in the ways that women and men are portrayed and the ways those who consume it view those people. The porn stars have indeed become objects themselves, and they dishonor their own humanity by allowing others to ignore their personhood for a price.

We also objectify men and women by equating them with certain roles. I saw a truck out on the street the other day with the name of a business written on its side: "Rent-a-Husband." As a single woman, I recognized immediately the need for such a business. I've said similar things when I've moaned to people that "I need a wife." I don't mean I have lesbian leanings but that I need someone to do the tasks traditionally associated with a wife like cooking, cleaning, and running errands.

But this kind of language turns people into objects, reducing a wife or husband to the performance of a particular function. This has always been a sore spot for me, and I ought to know better. I have never fit in with the roles traditionally associated with women. I avoid cooking whenever possible, get no satisfaction from cleaning, and have no real interest in handiwork. I value those things tremendously in others, but they don't interest me, and I get tired of people refusing me authority except in those areas.

I also remember a plane flight while I was serving my first church. When the man seated next to me discovered my profession, we got into quite an involved discussion about religion and Christian faith. It was an interesting discussion and the time on the flight went quickly. As the plane landed and we taxied to the gate, the man drew our conversation to a close with the words, "Well, I'm sure you're the prettiest pastor in town."

That one phrase took away all the pleasure of the conversation, although I'm sure he meant to be complimentary. I thought we were having an intellectual discussion about a common interest. His comment indicated his attention was elsewhere. As with racism, the issue of gender equity in this country has made some strides forward but much work remains. As a woman, I can now be ordained—but not in all churches. And, as a woman, I bump into the "stained-glass ceiling." Even in my own denomination, for instance, women are mostly appointed to the smaller churches with the lower salaries.

Reducing a person to their race, gender or any other particular attribute steals their right to be treated as a complete human being, with all the complexity and uniqueness that implies. We know better than that, and Christians especially should be able to do better. In Christ there is no male or female, black or white—we are all one in Christ Jesus.

■◉■◉■

"*The earth is the Lord's and all that is in it, the world and those who live in it.*" It is all God's. Every individual person. The earth itself and its resources. The animals, birds, fish, and insects. It's all God's. When we treat it as ours to use as we will, we have stolen not just from our neighbor, but from God, and have broken the eighth commandment.

False Witness

Thou shalt not bear false witness against thy neighbor.

The lie seems innocent at times. We even have a phrase for it . . . the "white lie." That's what I do when a little child brings me a paper full of scribbles and I say, "Why, that's beautiful!" But can a lie ever be truly innocent? My suspicion is that it cannot, as it seems that both Scripture and Christian theology have seen it as one of the fundamental building blocks of evil.

One of the things that really sparked my imagination in seminary was St. Augustine's argument that evil isn't a thing in and of itself. It's a lack. Like cold is the absence of heat and darkness the absence of light, so evil is the absence of good or of substance. When I have introduced that concept in Bible studies, some have objected, saying that calling evil very literally "no-thing" trivialized it with an "Oh, it's nothing" wave of the hand. But you can die of hypothermia, even though there's no actual thing called "cold."

Evil as a lack of something makes sense to me in a number of ways. To begin with, I don't have to spend time wondering why God created evil. Didn't happen. Evil is not a created thing. It's what you get when the created thing breaks down and leaves a void. The big crack in my ceiling wasn't put there by the builder, and the crack itself doesn't exist. If you took away the rest of the ceiling, it wouldn't be there. But because of that crack, the whole house could fall down on my head, even though the crack isn't a thing all by itself. You get the picture.

Evil as a lack also helps me better understand some of what Jesus has to say. In John 8:44, Jesus is chewing out the Pharisees. In a non-politically-correct moment he says:

> You are from your father the devil, and you choose to do your father's desires. He was a murderer from the beginning and does not stand in the truth, because there is no truth in him. When he lies, he speaks according to his own nature, for he is a liar and the father of lies.

A lie, too, is a lack—the absence of truth. Here in John, Jesus says the devil is characterized by the lie and that all lies have their origin in him. Then, just a few chapters later in John 14:6, Jesus calls himself the truth. Not just a truthful person, but as completely truth as the devil is completely lie. The devil is the lie, the thing that is not. Jesus is the truth, the one who is. Sounds kind of like Exodus 3:14, where God names himself "I am." God is defined by being, by substance. God is the one who is, over and against the idols who are not. When something turns out to be without substance it is a lie. The Bible seems to point to the lie as the most basic component of evil.

With that in mind, we can better understand why lying was important enough to make God's top ten list of sins. False witness is more than just a legal issue. It refers to lying and deceit in all its forms—witnessing to a reality that is false. It seems from both the Bible and Augustine that anything based in deceit is on a very slippery slope.

Of course much can be said about the devastating effect of lies in our personal lives and private relationships. But Christians should also be deeply involved in discussions about the systemic forms of false witness in our world. It may be hard for me to stay honest in all my personal interactions, but I am at least consciously making the choice either to be honest or to lie, which enables me to choose what's right, even though it may be hard.

Systemic lies are more difficult, however, because we're not always aware of them. Lies are told on our behalf by organizations, institutions, and corporations that have gained our trust. A company proclaims their product does no harm, when studies have shown otherwise. Bidding is rigged underneath a seemingly fair process. Money is supposedly going to help the unfortunate or to fund our pension when it is really lining an executive pocket. Perhaps the lie started with one person, but eventually the whole system comes to believe it is so. We can easily become swept up in a systemic lie that does incredible harm to others, while blissfully proclaiming our own righteousness. The papers are full of such stories, and it is time for Christians to start objecting when lying becomes an accepted part of any system to which we belong.

The Political System

"Propaganda is to a democracy what violence is to a dictatorship."
—William Blum, *Rogue State: A Guide to the World's Only Superpower* (Common Courage Press, 2000)

When I did a quick Internet search on the term "false witness," the majority of the hits dealt with political speech. We have come to the place where popular opinion believes that "honest politician" is an oxymoron. I don't believe politicians start out that way. Some may go into it for the ego trip or for some other unworthy motives, but I think most politicians began their careers with noble ideals and a desire to serve the public.

But as the political machine has grown and changed, it's taken on a life of its own, becoming a sometimes diabolical monster that eventually demands the human sacrifice of those who engage it. Every election seems to be worse, with all sides saying only what their constituents want to hear, whether it has any semblance to the truth or not. Responses are predictable, answers are partisan, and I get the feeling sometimes that if I reached out and poked the air with a hatpin, the whole thing would pop and be seen to be nothing at all—a deficiency or lack of being—a lie.

We like to blame politicians for this, and they do bear some responsibility. But part of the reason politicians feel such behavior is necessary is because of us—the voters who want what we want, when we want it, without any personal cost. The painful truth is that if politicians told the truth to us, we wouldn't elect them. They know that. They want the job and do whatever it takes. So whoever offers us a free ride most convincingly is in. Whoever makes us feel good is in. Whoever demands the least from us is in. "Take up your cross and follow me" isn't a winning political strategy, even if it might be the only way out of our mess.

The issue is that Christians are sacrificing themselves to the machine. Christians haven't had this much involvement in political life since the civil rights era, but this time around we seem to be more interested in playing the game ourselves rather than making sure others are playing the game fairly. We've become as partisan as anyone else, confusing loyalty to God with loyalty to nation and loyalty to nation with loyalty to a particular party or person. Like the rest of the country, we want to have our pork and eat it, too.

It would be more helpful to stop blaming either one another, or politicians, and realize that the political beast that has consumed our unity and spit us out piecemeal is a beast of our own making. As Americans, we've all made that beast. We trained it, and we feed it daily. Now it has turned on us and instead of examining our own consciences, we blame those we hired to guard the cage.

Those concerned about the ninth commandment should be troubled not only that we have some corrupt politicians who lie to us, but that we have an entire political system that makes telling the full truth almost impossible. And that's just the effect of our own personal sins on the electoral system.

Part of what we insist on hearing from those seeking election is that the United States lives up to the ideals of our Constitution, our patriotic songs, and our icons, including the Statue of Liberty, lifting her lamp beside the "golden door." Politicians who might honestly want to challenge that view are painted as unpatriotic and therefore unelectable. Christians who care about truth need to become courageous enough to open up that golden door and look inside.

Espionage

Formed by an act of Congress in 1947, the CIA was authorized by the National Security Council to undertake covert action. Covert means secret, and the bigger the secret, the more likely it is that you'll have to lie in order to keep it. That's what spying is all about.

Nobody thinks the covert operations of the CIA operate honestly and openly—being dishonest is the whole point. With the creation of the CIA, the United States decided that the ends justify the means and that there are times when nations should use citizens to lie on their behalf. Though it may be in the national interest, that's not the point. The point is that the national interest and the Christian interest are not interchangeable. So, my first question is, "How should Christians react to the fact that we have a huge government agency with a major function dedicated to the practice of false witness?"

As a person who has accepted the covenant of the Ten Commandments, how am I to respond to that fact? Could I work as a spy and retain my faith? Should I be lobbying for the dissolution of the CIA since the threat it was created to address (Communism) has all but vanished? As I started to research this issue, the questions got much bigger as the golden door opened to reveal some truly disturbing scenes.

In his 1978 book *In Search of Enemies,* former CIA official John Stockwell records words from the Hoover Commission report of 1954 in talking about the role of U.S. espionage in facing the rising communist threat:

> There are no rules in such a game. Hitherto acceptable norms of human conduct do not apply. If the U.S. is to survive, long-standing American concepts of "fair play" must be reconsidered. We must develop effective espionage and counterespionage services. We must learn to subvert, sabotage and destroy our enemies by more clever, more sophisticated and more effective methods than those used against us. It may become necessary that the American people be acquainted with, understand and support this fundamentally repugnant philosophy.[1]

Ouch. Here's another glimpse from former CIA officer, now professor at Boston University, Arthur Hulnick:

> Professional standards require intelligence professionals to lie, hide information, or use covert tactics to protect their "cover," access, sources, and responsibilities. The Central Intelligence Agency expects, teaches, encourages, and controls these tactics so that the lies are consistent and supported ("backstopped"). The CIA expects intelligence officers to teach others to lie, deceive, steal, launder money, and perform a variety of other activities that would certainly be illegal if practiced in the United States. They call these tactics "tradecraft," and intelligence officers practice them in all the world's intelligence services.[2]

And then there's the recruitment of agents in foreign countries. Some become agents willingly, sometimes out of legitimate dissatisfaction with an oppressive or tyrannical regime. Others are attracted to the mystique of the "spy," or the promise of extra income.

But, as Faust would tell you, there is a price to playing the devil's game. Volunteer agents can find that they are lied to as well, with many being considered "expendable" for the larger cause. The end justifies the means in this game, after all. And those are the willing agents.

There are also those agents who have been recruited through deception, coercion, and blackmail. Check out this information from H.H.A. Cooper, the former staff director for the Task Force on Disorders and Terrorism:

> Those cultivating the spy will press favors upon him, without, in the initial stages, asking for anything in return. This is clearly a matter in which sensibilities must be catered to in order to avoid giving offense or having one's motives suspect. Reciprocity obliges most people to respond in kind; the trick is to escalate the exchange to the point where a more compromising engagement can be undertaken.[3]

You've just read instructions on how to corrupt an innocent person—how to manipulate someone into doing things they have believed to be unethical and immoral so that we might use them as an agent. Once they have been convinced to act illegally or immorally, they can be blackmailed into ever greater illicit activity.

Further, David Perry, Professor of Ethics at the U.S. Army War College reports this:

> For at least two decades the Agency funded experiments using mind-altering drugs, electroshock, hypnosis, sensory deprivation, and other techniques in an elusive quest to find foolproof ways to manipulate agents.[4]

Perry also quotes from *Thwarting Enemies at Home and Abroad: How to Be a Counterintelligence Officer* by former Intelligence Officer William R. Johnson:

> [P]hysical pain is not relevant in interrogation. Anxiety, humiliation, loneliness, and pride are another story. . . . The person who enjoys hurting is a lousy interrogator in even the most humane situation. But the humane person who shrinks from manipulating his subject is also a lousy interrogator. . . . The interrogator, like a priest or doctor [!], must have a talent for empathy, a personal need to communicate with other people, a concern for what makes other people tick even when he is putting maximum emotional pressure on them.[5]

Now what are Christians supposed to do with that?

I've used so many quotes because it's more compelling to hear former officers in their own words. The CIA is not a rogue organization. It's an official government agency. The tax dollars of Christians support its activities, and those who claim Christian faith work within its ranks.

To be fair, some CIA work is completely benign. John Stockwell describes the CIA's Deputy Directorate of Information:

> [The DOI fulfills] the mission outlined in the National Security Act of 1947 of centralizing all of the raw intelligence available to our government, collating it, analyzing it for meaning and importance, and relaying finished reports to the appropriate offices. . . The "DDI is overt—its employees are openly 'CIA' to friends, relatives, neighbors, and creditors; it is passive; and it is benign, without aggressive activity which can harm anyone."[6]

I don't mean to suggest that there are no legitimate functions or decent, moral folks at the CIA. It is the covert operations that seem problematic.

Stockwell believes that the covert operations of the CIA are not essential to our national interest and, in fact, haven't worked very well.[7] That may or may not be true, but such tactics are not what God intended for nations as they deal with other nations, and although they may be legal, such operations violate more than just the ninth commandment.

The difficult issue at the root of it all is not whether such tactics work, but how Christians engage a society where the way of the lie is an officially sanctioned method of dealing with other countries. And what if the tactics *did* work? It's the same as the torture question. Can the ends ever justify the means? Is it okay for a Christian to torture someone just because they don't enjoy legal protection? What if sticking to our own principles put not only ourselves, but our whole nation at risk? What would Jesus do? Moral issues are complex and have far-reaching implications.

We Christians today mostly have lost our moral courage. The earliest Christians seriously examined how they could and couldn't engage the culture around them. When they took on the mantle of baptism, they threw off many of society's privileges and possibilities and took on an often persecuted status.

Justin Martyr, a second-century convert to Christianity, describes the Christians of the time this way:

> We must then offer no resistance. He [Jesus] never wanted us to imitate the wicked. Rather, he challenged us to lead everyone away from shamefulness and pleasure in evil by patience and kindness. We can in fact show that many who were once among you have been transformed in this way. They gave up their violent and domineering ways. Either they were conquered by the sight of their neighbors' patient

life, or they were convinced by noticing the extraordinary kindness and patience of some defrauded traveling companions, or they were overcome by encountering and testing this attitude in people with whom they had business dealings. Anyone who is not found living in accordance with his teaching should not be regarded as a Christian even if he confesses to Christ's teaching with his lips. For he said that only those shall be saved who do not just talk, but who also do the corresponding works.[8]

He also describes the price that they paid for such behavior:

We do not give up our confession though we be executed by the sword, though we be crucified, thrown to wild beasts, put in chains, and exposed to fire and every other kind of torture. Everyone knows this. On the contrary, the more we are persecuted and martyred, the more do others in ever-increasing numbers become believers and God-fearing people through the name of Jesus.[9]

It was in that way and at such cost that the early Christians transformed the cultures in which they lived. That was how they faced down the false, exploitative and violent systems of the ancient world. How will Christians do that today?

The Legal System

Ironically, one of the hardest places to discern the truth is in a courtroom. Lawyers tend to get most of the blame for this. You've all heard the lawyer jokes. A 2005 Gallup poll found that only 18 percent of Americans rate lawyers as having "high ethical standards."[10] A Columbia Law School nationwide survey found "almost two-thirds of Americans think lawyers are overpaid, about half think attorneys do more harm than good, and four in ten think lawyers are dishonest."[11] And yet we now have a society where you can't even die without one.

I personally know ethical lawyers and Christian judges who live out their faith. I know the patience and forbearance of a defense attorney whose client stole his car while he was defending the client in another case. During my time in seminary in the early 1990s, I did my field work at the Justice Center of Atlanta, where I was trained as a conflict mediator and where I mediated cases for two years. I spent many days in a city courtroom, waiting for cases that the judge would refer for mediation.

I saw a lot. I saw the racial and class inequities. I saw the overburdened judges trying to be fair to people who, as far as I was concerned, deserved a good, swift kick. I also saw judges who didn't listen, and one who sat back in his chair and tossed his gavel around in a juggling game with himself as people tried to make their case.

I have also done volunteer work inside jails and prisons. I've had my life threatened by an inmate and have been invited to a hotel room by a prison official to "make my case" for an inmate's rights. I've been to court with church members who have been both rightly and wrongly accused of crimes—some serious, some minor. In short, I've been around the legal system on a number of sides, and I can say only two things for sure: there exist both the best and the worst of intentions in every sector, and our legal system has abandoned justice for the sake of the law.

We've all known of the cases where key pieces of evidence can't be used in a trial because they were obtained without a search warrant or without following some other technicality. So, it's okay to use the "waterboarding" technique (where suspects are forced underwater to the point they believe they will drown) to get information we need as a nation, but the jury can't hear the taped confession of the man who buried little Jessica Lunsford alive because the taped confession was obtained improperly? We can bribe, coerce, and extort foreign nationals to break their own laws and give us intelligence, but we can't talk about the heroin stash found in the defendant's home because the information was obtained without a search warrant? We operate on two extremes, and neither seems to have much to do with justice.

It's true we have a "legal system," but it is false witness to say we have any sort of large-scale mechanism for justice in America. This is true even with juries. We've all heard the jury instructions where citizens are told the limits on the verdicts they can issue and, in states where there are sentencing guidelines, what sentence a judge can impose. "If you can't definitively prove x, then you can't say y." There's little room for either spirit or creativity and thus no room for true justice.

Those sorts of boundaries made the process of mediation, an alternative to the adversarial win/lose court system, appeal to me. In that process, regular citizens could be trained as mediators, and lawyers were actively discouraged from attending mediation sessions with their clients. A good friend of mine who was an attorney before coming to seminary found that she constantly had to push back her training as a lawyer in order to do the very different work of mediation.

Mediation provided the opportunity to find out what was at the bottom of a complaint. Those coming for mediation knew the process was confidential. Telling the truth to me couldn't harm a case if it ended up back in court, and it might well resolve the problem. So they told the truth. I can't speak for others, but in my cases, the cases almost never went back to court.

There's a lot of talk of tort reform these days—cleaning up the mess of frivolous lawsuits and ambulance-chasing attorneys while still trying to protect those who have legitimately been harmed by negligent or malicious individuals and corporations. When I started to do research on tort reform, I immediately saw that it was as politically polarized as everything else. To demand caps on damage awards is code for "vote GOP" and pointing out that the large corporations who benefit from those caps contribute generously to Republicans is written into the script of every Democrat.

Both are right. There are tort abuses that lead to the further erosion of our legal integrity and there is a need for independent watchdogs to be sure that any tort reform legislation is not merely license for corporations and institutions to behave however they please without restraint. But there is a third way: true mediation.

What I saw in my two years of mediating astounded me. When I saw the entrenched positions of those who came in and what was being demanded as a resolution, I often thought there would be no way to reach any mutual agreement. As time went on, however, I generally found that the issue on the table wasn't the real issue. The court system, in about 8 out of 10 cases that I dealt with, was being used as a vehicle simply to make someone listen.

The mediation structure allowed for each side to state their case, uninterrupted, while the other side listened. They weren't guided in their statement by my specific questions, they weren't limited in their responses. They simply told their story from their point of view. Then they sat and listened to the other side. In many cases, this was the first time such listening had happened. The prior talk had often gone only through lawyers.

Then I'd meet privately with each side as the other side waited in another room. In these discussions I often found out the longer history and the larger issues. The theft by conversion was really a divorce case. The money being requested was a way to get the other side to acknowledge a wrong done. And so it went. Lastly, we got back together to see if some sort of common ground could be found.

The role of forgiveness in this process was enormous. I watched people give up literally tens of thousands of dollars, money that a judge probably would have awarded to them if they went back to court, just because the other side extended a hand and said, "I had no idea I had hurt you that way. I'm sorry." When we could get down to the real issues, we could come up with real solutions. When real listening happened, real repentance and forgiveness could take place.

That couldn't happen under the usual legal protocols. Saying "I'm sorry" is an admission of guilt that lawyers generally advise their clients to avoid. "I'm sorry" is a sign of weakness, and the other side is ready to pounce when those words are spoken. But in the protected space of mediation we could get beyond mere legalities and deal with the true issues of justice.

Various levels of government are beginning to develop certification standards and guidelines for mediation. Some areas require that mediators be attorneys, others provide training to anyone. National standards that allow for mediators who are not immersed or invested in the win/lose culture of our current legal system would be a giant step forward.

Seminaries could be more actively involved in the mediation process. Just as a person needing counseling today can choose between a regular counselor and a minister with special training as a pastoral counselor, so someone in conflict could choose between a regular mediator and a seminary graduate trained as a pastoral mediator. Those in faith communities who believe in both truth and justice could follow a calling to be trained by the state or in universities and given good careers as mediators, helping to relieve a legal system crushed by an overload of cases, and helping to restore some humanity to a process where humanity is often lacking.

Domestic Abuse[12]

I had been in my first church about two weeks. It was about 11 p.m. and I heard gunshots and screams. An ambulance came to the house across the street and took away a young man I'll call Mark. His brother-in-law,

Mo, had blown Mark's arm off with a shotgun, kept loaded under the bed even though a second-grader lived in the house.

Mo's wife, Dianne, was distraught as she learned her brother's arm would have to be amputated. None of them went to my church, but a relative did, and so I ended up providing pastoral support. I sat with Dianne during Mark's surgery. Mo did not come, but he called Dianne every few minutes, demanding that she leave the hospital and come home to be with him. Every time he called, she became more and more upset, until finally I had her hand the phone to me.

"Miss Anne," said Mo, "she's my wife and I want her here. I've got the right to have her where I want her. Don't the Bible say that she's got to listen to me?" It was all I could do to contain myself.

"No," I said. "It doesn't. You're fine and Mark's arm is being amputated. She needs to be here with her brother."

Mo was furious. "She has to come home!"

"No, she doesn't." I said. He hung up. I called the police officer who lived next door and asked him to keep an eye on my house and my dog, and then Dianne and I had a talk. It all began to come out—Mo trying to keep Dianne away from family and friends, Mo beating Dianne whenever he felt like it, Dianne thinking if she could only learn to please Mo that he would stop hurting her . . . thinking it was her fault . . . Mo begging to be given another chance if Dianne threatened to leave. She always gave him another chance. The situation never changed.

But now it had escalated and Mo had seriously hurt a member of her family. What about her son? What about the dog? She didn't know what to do. We talked off and on for weeks. I gave her numbers for shelters and tried everything I knew of to get her to leave. She kept going back. "I'll just have to act better," she would say. "Then he'll stop. It's my fault. I shouldn't make him angry."

Finally I said to her, "Dianne, is it okay to push God's child down the stairs and then smash her head into a wall?"

"No!" she said at once.

"You are God's child," I told her. "What he is doing to you is wrong. It's not okay. God doesn't like it." It was a bit of truth-telling, and it did the trick. Once Dianne saw herself as she truly was—as a child of God rather than as the chattel Mo had named her—her spirit was free. It was not easy, but it made her willing to take the steps necessary to get herself and her son to safety.

Mo's violent behavior was false witness. It was telling the world that he owned his wife as a piece of property. He was proclaiming that he owned her and could do whatever he wanted to her and to her family. He was saying that she didn't matter, that her own wants and needs were invalid and unimportant and that the Bible sanctioned such attitudes in saying that wives needed to be submissive to their husbands. It was a lie.

Dianne is not alone. In 2001 there were 588,490 women and 103,220 men who reported violence from an intimate partner,[13] and it is broadly assumed that both statistics are vastly underreported, even though women are 7 to 14 times more likely to report severe physical assaults from an intimate partner.[14]

Dianne was also lucky. In 2000 alone, 1,247 women and 440 men were killed by an intimate partner.[15] Homicide is the leading cause of death for pregnant and recently pregnant women.[16] I have known women who were facing such death threats because the child's father didn't want to have to pay child support. "Get an abortion or I'll kill you" was a real threat heard by women I knew from men who meant it. So, do be careful in your rush to judge those who have abortions and your eagerness to cut off access. The problem is complex.

Violence in homes isn't limited to spousal abuse. In 2002, child protective agencies confirmed 906,000 children in the United States as being maltreated.[17] Those are the confirmed ones. An estimated 1,500 died from maltreatment.[18] Any shelter will tell you that when there is violence in the home, it is likely that everyone living there is at risk—spouse, children, pets.

It is well past time for Christians to start telling the truth about what goes on in too many American homes. This isn't an outside-the-church problem. Nor is it restricted by race or class. In every church I've served, I've dealt with this issue. I have also heard too many pastors address it by sending victims back to their abusers for the sake of keeping the family together.

The Church needs to stop bearing the false witness that this doesn't happen in our midst and name the truth that this is sin. If violence against the unborn is a horror to God, how much more violence against those already born in the image of God and walking the earth? We do not own people. Every creature on the earth belongs to God. We are stewards of one another, especially those in our household. Mutual submission is what Paul calls for in Ephesians 5, not domination and certainly not harm.

Nearly one-third of American women report being physically or sexually abused by a husband or boyfriend at some point in their lives.[19] Look around your congregation. It is happening there. Forty percent of girls age 14 to 17 report knowing someone their age who has been hit or beaten by a boyfriend.[20] Those who seek to protect the family should be leading the charge on this issue.

In too many states, reporting domestic abuse is a road to nowhere except more of the same from a now angrier abuser. In too many places restraining orders have no teeth. In almost every state, agencies that deal with child abuse are underfunded and case loads are so huge there's no way to really protect even the children who are reported, let alone to search out the others.

According to the Chicago Tribune, the National Rifle Association's annual budget for 2004 was $180 million. Wouldn't it be a wonderful gesture if some of that money could support the shelters housing those running from gun violence? Wouldn't it be great if those who insist that everyone should be able to carry automatic weapons paid the medical costs of the innocent victims of those weapons?

Why aren't churches more vocal on this issue? It's not like we're intent on staying out of people's bedrooms. We're shouting about sexual promiscuity all the time. What about sexual abuse? We're finally starting to speak out about the pedophiles, but what about the woman in one of the churches I served whose husband demanded sexual acts at gunpoint? How is she to respond to your Ephesians 5, wives-submit-to-your-husbands sermon? And what about the deacon I knew in a Baptist church? I sat with his children and watched as his wife threw a television at him. What support does he have?

Christians have proven they can organize to achieve legislative goals, at least for things that we care about. Why don't we seem to care about this one? Maybe we prefer the false witness that all the families in our churches are happy and nice to each other. It's time to tell the truth and face the issue.

Of course in speaking about "false witness," it should be said that there are those who seek to destroy others by making false accusations. Especially in the area of child molestation, a person is branded for life just by the accusation, even if it should be proven false. Both of my parents worked in the public schools. I remember the sense of fearful horror that descended on our living room when they heard the news that all the middle school students had been given a hotline where they could anonymously report abuse by teachers. My parents were counselors and knew the realities of abuse. But they also knew the realities of adolescence and that bringing down a hated teacher with one anonymous phone call would prove too much of a temptation for some.

They also remembered the fate of a family friend. He had been a teacher in the same school until the fateful day that he bought some pipe tobacco and sat in his car to stuff his pipe, holding the pipe in his lap. Some teenage girls came by, took a glance in the car window, mistook the pipe for something else and charged him with indecent exposure. The charge was later dropped—but he lost his job. A core principle of the American legal system has been that a person is innocent until proven guilty. Our abuse laws need to be strict and justice swift for those who harm the innocents. But we also need to be careful that our zeal in enforcement doesn't end up creating a vengeful haven for the false witness.

Illegal Immigration

A Korean colleague tells the story of his young daughter who one day got hold of his wallet. She began to go through the contents and came across his driver's license. It was stamped "Resident alien." With eyes bulging from their sockets, she went up to the father she thought she knew, visions of spaceships in her head, and said, "Dad, are you really an alien?"

I've often wondered why, especially in our politically correct world, calling someone an "alien," whether legal or otherwise, isn't challenged. The word has a negative connotation. Like my friend's daughter, we think of aliens as not quite human—beings from another planet who have come here for reasons we don't know but suspect are harmful. Why are we using that word?

Well, it is biblical. The Bible talks a lot about aliens, who are even mentioned in the Ten Commandments—they are to be given a Sabbath like everybody else. Other protective verses like Exodus 22:21 proclaim: "You shall not wrong or oppress a resident alien, for you were aliens in the land of Egypt." The Bible calls them "aliens." Or does it?

I wanted to see the various contexts where the Bible used the word "alien," so I turned to my trusty concordance software. My research led me down a much different path. What the New Revised Standard Version called an "alien," the King James simply termed a "stranger." Sometime between the publication of the King James in 1611 and the twentieth-century production of the NRSV, "strangers" became "aliens" to us.

That may seem like just semantics, but as a people of the Word, we should recognize that the words we use are important. "Stranger" in our language and culture is simply someone we don't know. It doesn't imply a non-human status or a lack of belonging. A stranger is full of possibility. We teach children to be wary of strangers, but we have all had the experience of being a stranger ourselves and know that a stranger is just as likely to be a potential friend as a potential threat.

I don't know why there was such a significant shift in the language of the two translations, but I'd love to see the term "alien" go away. "Foreign national" works just fine, as does "immigrant," or perhaps some other term. What we call people, however, is only one of the issues surrounding immigration, both legal and non, in our country; and the reason that I have put this issue under the commandment not to bear false witness is because of New York Harbor.

I graduated from high school in 1976, the bicentennial of our nation. My home state of Rhode Island put together a bicentennial youth choir of which I was a part, and we had a whole repertoire of patriotic songs. I don't remember the title, but one of those songs contained part of the poem "The New Colossus" by the Jewish American poet Emma Lazarus. That poem is engraved on the pedestal of the Statue of Liberty, which for so long was the sentinel that greeted immigrants to this country. Singing those words was the first time I had really paid attention to them, and they stay with me still, especially the last lines: "Give me your tired, your poor, your huddled masses yearning to breathe free, the wretched refuse of your teeming shore. Send these, the homeless, tempest-tost to me, I lift my lamp beside the golden door."

Maybe we have never really lived by that standard. But I do know we're not living by it now. When the "huddled masses yearning to breathe free" pile in a boat and head for the Florida coast, the Coast Guard catches them and turns them back. When the tired and poor struggle across our southern border into the desert, we arrest them and send them back (often in body bags), complaining to their governments that we don't want "the wretched refuse of your teeming shores."

I know there are real issues. With smugglers and terrorists coming across our borders, we need security. There are issues with jobs, and language, and taking in "the homeless, tempest-tost" puts a very real strain on limited resources. I know that. But perhaps we should have thought of those things before we put the Statue of Liberty in our harbor and announced our open arms to the world.

The issue of the strangers in our land is really the issue of the stranger in our churches writ large. Churches everywhere give lip service to wanting to reach out to welcome the tired, the poor. Some even start programs to reach them. But very few churches are prepared for the reality of a congregation full of tired, poor people. I have watched resentment build because the poor cannot financially support the programs they need and use. The tired don't have the energy to serve on a committee or help with a supper. The "wretched refuse of the teeming shores" of our neighborhoods often bring poor judgment, unruly children, and few social skills right into our clean, orderly church buildings and services. It isn't long before we put policies in place that serve as effective barriers to keep them out.

We want to have our cake and eat it, too. Both as churches and as a nation, we want the image of reaching out to the underprivileged with open arms. We want the world to love us and for the underdog to see us as the "land of opportunity," the place so much better than their home country that everyone will want to come here. But we don't want to deal with the problems when they do come here.

Part of our solution has simply been to export America. I'm not just talking about outsourcing jobs, but to push the American ethos, along with democracy and capitalism, into every other country. If they become like us, they won't have to come here. Except that philosophy doesn't honor the indigenous cultures of other nations and peoples. It's an offensive and arrogant policy, but when other nations tell us that, we bristle that they "hate freedom."

We have a promise to the world sitting in New York Harbor. If we don't intend to keep that promise, we should send the statue back to France and apologize to the world for making a promise we couldn't keep. If we do want to find a way to keep the promise, we need to quit blaming the "homeless, tempest-tost" who come here and look to the causes of their homelessness and poverty.

Sometimes those causes can be linked directly back to us. We have plundered the resources of other nations, imposed crippling debt, taken advantage of cheap labor, let free trade rather than fair trade rule, and contributed to climate changes that worsen their droughts and storms. Despite rampant corruption in some of the nations to our south, we have not seemed as intent on forcing change in those places as we have with nations more strategically important to us.

Suppose we worked on stopping the unjust practices that create poverty in other nations? In the long-term that seems to me a better solution than refusing a driver's license or job to someone whose only crime is believing what we promised them.

But no matter what a person proposes for solutions to illegal immigration, the Christian must remain vigilant lest our concerns about a person's legal status lead us down the ugly path of hatred and racism. "Illegal immigrant" is a political status, not a moral category. Every person who crosses our borders is made in the image of God, whether they have a visa or not. We invited them here; we exploited them when they came; and now we must deal with the mess we have made, atone for our own sins, and come up with a solution that is both merciful and just. Those who worship a just and merciful God should have a voice in that.

■O■O■

Telling the truth is hard for all of us. It's hard even to go through one day without getting caught up in whether I should really tell the truth as I see it, if I should let a rumor go unchallenged, or to really see if I have misrepresented my opinion as fact or exaggerated something for my own advantage.

As the issues get more difficult, with more at stake, it's harder still. Gays and lesbians debate revealing the truth of their sexual orientation. A seminary friend reported that people who worked in abuse shelters (for both people and animals) lied almost daily to get someone out of harm's way.

Yet we sit with the biblical implication that the lie is where evil begins. We sit with a commandment not to bear false witness. It seems to me that the lies we came to accept in our personal lives as being "white lies"—those little lapses done for the sake of the greater good—have led us to a larger complacency. Now there are federal institutions like the CIA where lying is the expectation and so much a part of doing business that revealing the truth about an undercover agent is a federal crime. No, we shouldn't "out" all of our agents—too many lives are at stake. But when we come to a point where telling the truth is a crime, something has gone terribly wrong.

Little lies grow to big ones and individual lies grow to corporate ones. We might regain a culture of truth the same way. Maybe if Christians focused on telling the small truths, they would grow to bigger truths. Maybe if we began with deep reflection on individual truth-telling, it would grow to corporate truth-telling. Maybe if we were willing to hear the truth from our friends we could become willing to hear the truth from politicians. And if we were willing to hear it without tossing them out of office, maybe they would be willing to tell it.

And if they could tell the truth to their constituents, maybe they could tell the truth to each other, to the lobbyists, and to government agencies. Christians are supposed to be a people of hope. We hope in Jesus who said in John 8:32: "You will know the truth, and the truth will make you free." I think it's worth a try.

10

Thou Shalt Not Covet

Thou shalt not covet they neighbor's house, thou shalt not covet thy neighbor's wife, nor his manservant, nor his maidservant, nor his ox, nor his ass, nor any thing that is thy neighbor's.

As I understand it, Buddhism revolves around the eradication of coveting, a focus Christians might do well to imitate. If you're not going to focus on the first of the Ten Commandments, you might do far worse than turning to the last. The Hebrew word for covet, *chamad*, means to desire. While I can't quite envision a world without any forms of desire, it does seem to me that, in America at least, our desires are completely out of control.

No one appears exempt. We've all seen the temper tantrums of the very young whose desires for things in the candy aisle are being thwarted. Otherwise normal, kind parents become monsters when it comes to fighting off other parents to score the toy du jour at Christmas. I knew a woman once who cried to me that her salary was too low and she couldn't make ends meet, while at home her dining room table was covered with packages ordered from catalog houses and shopping networks that had never even been opened, let alone used.

Those are extreme examples, but I know the problem intimately. I always wonder at those bastions of self-control who are able to engage in window shopping. I can't do that. Inevitably I will see something that I like and decide that life simply can't go on without it—though it's gone on without it quite nicely until that moment. Others have the ability to walk by and admire. I admire too, but my admiration turns to desire and the next thing I know, I'm getting a loan to consolidate my credit card debt. Others are in jail for shoplifting.

It is not just an economic phenomenon. The same principle moves someone from admiration to lust to rape or adultery. It moves us from thoughts of vengeance to the desire to see another punished to murder. The desire for more time to do things leads us to abandon the Sabbath, which leaves us with no energy to take on the difficult task of honoring our parents. Coveting is the attitude of the heart that precedes the breaking of all the other commandments, just as putting God first is the attitude that helps us keep them.

Advertising

Maybe this is naive, but it seems to me that advertising began as a very legitimate means of telling others about a product or service. It was information that answered three basic questions: What is it? What does it do? Where can I get it? I still see that sort of advertising. It's on signs stapled to phone poles or trees that say, "Yards mowed. $35. Call Steve." I haven't seen an innocent ad on television in—well, I don't know how long.

Advertising now is aimed at creating desire and eliminating the need for patience or self-control. Often the desire created isn't even for the item or service being sold. I have a desire for a particular brand of car because I want to be one of the beautiful, carefree people in the ad. That is my true desire. I'm not buying a vehicle to get me from here to there. I'm buying an image of myself that I can project to the world for a price, even if it is not at all true.

Not only do we buy things we don't need or don't even want in order to obtain the false image, we buy things that actually do us harm. We don't have to get deep or profound with this, we simply have to look at women's shoes. The back and foot problems of women who force their feet into unnatural shapes and heights are well documented. But I don't see many tennis shoes or Mary Janes on Oscar night. As I write this the new fashion is promoting loafers with three-inch heels. Hello? You can't loaf in three-inch heels. But we buy them and suffer like Cinderella's stepsisters because we covet the image.

And then there are the pharmaceuticals. The ads for hair-growth products mystified me because I couldn't figure out what the product was supposed to do. Everything was implied, and the implication was that you could get better jobs and have better relationships if you bought it.

Once I figured out what it was for, I noticed that it wasn't a product you could actually go out and buy. You had to convince your doctor to prescribe it for you. Soon the doors were flung open wide and drugs for every possible condition were being advertised on television—drugs you couldn't buy without the cooperation of your doctor.

This seems like one of the most dangerous turns in advertising ever. I want a doctor prescribing medicine for me because it is the drug I need, not because I'm begging for a life like the people in an ad. To be honest, I don't even really want the doctor prescribing it because I'm becoming more cynical about the influence of pharmaceutical companies on the medical profession. I want the pharmacist to tell me what I need—not because a company is throwing money at her to promote a drug, but because it's medically the best choice for my condition and has the least chance for harmful side effects. Pharmacists are in the best position to know this. A TV ad is not.

Advertising is a moral issue because it promotes the violation of the tenth commandment. Marketers are paid to sell products, not to actually improve your life. They don't get a commission based on how many successful relationships you have using Cialis. They get paid to make you convince your doctor to prescribe it. People who create ads don't get paid according to the number of times you actually use a product. Their pay isn't based on the product's success. They get paid by making you think you can't possibly live another minute without it and by ringing up the sale.

I saw this in a small way when I was in high school, working a job in an ice cream shop. A customer would order a root beer float, and there were very specific directions on how to prepare it. I was to fill a tall glass with root beer and then put a nice large scoop of ice cream on the rim of the glass.

As you might imagine, I had more cleaning to do at these tables than at others, and one day I said to my supervisor, "There must be some other way to serve floats. Nobody can eat them. There's not enough room in the glass to put the ice cream down into the root beer, and if they start to eat it off the rim, it falls off."

"That's not our concern," he said. "It looks good, so people will buy it. Your job is just to make sure the ice cream doesn't fall off before the customer touches it."

That's the principle behind almost all advertising and that's a moral issue. Not only has it led us to build an economy on a house of cards, as we ratchet up our acquisition of unneeded items to record highs, but it creates huge levels of discontent over unsatisfied desires. Discontent leads to anger, which gets turned inward to eating disorders, depression, and suicide or outward to sexual predation, stealing, road rage, and murder. The subtleties of advertising convince us that some kinds of people are worthwhile while others are not, that we can buy happiness, and that the satisfaction of our every desire is a fundamental human right. That is false witness, as well as coveting, and it harms the children of God.

The Earth's Resources

I've said it before and I'll say it again: God didn't give us ownership of the earth. Psalm 24 tells us that the earth and all that is in it is the Lord's. We are stewards—not owners. Resources aren't available for us to use however we like, but in accordance with the wishes and directives of the owner.

That's not to say that it's never okay to extract oil or coal from the bowels of the earth or to use the wood of the forest to build a house or a table. It *is* to say that the mere existence of an oil field doesn't give us permission to drill it, and the presence of a tree or the need for more homes doesn't give us the right to raze a forest. It's not to say we can never eat meat, but the deplorable conditions in which so many farm animals are kept so that profits can be higher is covetousness at its most disgusting.

Again, the root of the abuse of the earth, from over-fishing to drilling in sensitive ecological areas, is the desire to have what we want and to have it immediately. If I don't like the feel or look of recycled paper, I should be able to use something else. If there is oil to be tapped somewhere, I shouldn't have to change my lifestyle to consume less. If my business can make more money by getting rid of air quality controls, then I should be free of those regulations.

We can justify our covetousness quite well. More money for my business means more jobs, which means a better economy, which means everybody is happy. Because it's the economy, stupid. It's not about what's moral or just. It's not about what God has instructed but about what money will do.

The breaking of this commandment leads to breaking God's commandments for the earth and animals to have a Sabbath (Lev 25). When we use the resources of God's earth without heed for the practices God has designed, it's only a small step to using God's "human resources" in a similar manner, resulting in abominable labor conditions, the lack of a living wage, unfair trade practices, and the ultimate in deplorable practices, slavery.

In this area as well, our covetousness leads to stealing, as we steal the resources of other nations around the globe. Where are Africa's diamonds? How many unholy alliances have we made for the sake of oil? How many have died? Why are God's elephants and tigers and polar bears disappearing from the earth? Why are the plankton in the ocean and the glaciers of the north disappearing? As God comes walking in the Garden at the cool of the day, God may well turn to us again and say, "What is this that you have done?" (Gen 3:13).

For too long Christians have turned a blind eye to our role as stewards of God's earth. Those cattle on a thousand hills don't belong to any rancher or dairy farmer. They belong to God. Check it out in Psalm 50. In that same Psalm God lays claim to every beast of the forest. They are God's, and God worked hard to create both a home for them and a completely amazing ecosystem that would keep it all in balance. We move into their homes without asking and then exterminate them because we don't want them living with us. "Can't have panthers in my back yard—they're dangerous!" Well, who says they have to be the ones to move? Who says we have a right to live wherever we desire—on whatever property we covet without regard to whatever or whoever is already living there?

Again, this is not to say we can never develop land, but that even Christians have forgotten who owns the earth and all that dwell therein. How many developers—even Christian developers—pray about whether a given tract of land should be altered? How many Christian foresters stop and ask God whether logging in this particular area is in accordance with God's wishes? How many Christians owning an industrial complex ask God about what environmental controls should be installed at their plant?

Biodiversity

The word "biodiversity" refers to the enormous complexity and interdependence of life on earth in all its forms. It's about the different kinds of ecosystems—how the environments around mountains are different from coastal areas, for example. It's about the 13 million or so different species of animals, plants, and microorganisms that exist on the earth as well as the genetic differences within those species. It's about all of life and how all of life interacts.

As Christians, we believe that God designed all of that, and we can safely assume that, whatever the specifics of God's will, generally God wants the systems to run as God created them to run. For a long time, we didn't even know we were dealing with systems and thought that whatever we did in the environment had no effect beyond what we could see with our eyes. We were very wrong.

Now we know that mountains aren't just very pretty and really cool to climb up or to ski down. Research has shown us that 30 to 60 percent of downstream fresh water comes from mountains.[1] And that's just in the humid areas. In dry areas the percentage goes up to 70 to 90 percent.[2] That's fresh water for drinking, cooking, and washing, but also for industry, hydroelectricity, and agriculture as well as the plant and animal species that only live in mountainous environments. Mountains matter. You can't just strip mine them, take all their trees, or turn them into resorts without serious side effects.

And it's not just mountains. Every environment on earth—the coastal areas, the deserts, and so on—has unique gifts to offer us, and contributions to our well-being that we're only just beginning to understand.

We talk about "frozen wastelands" because those areas aren't useful to us—or so we think. Our "frozen wastelands" are disappearing, and it's a cause for concern. A report by the World Wildlife Fund claims that "average global temperatures are expected to rise 1.4 to 5.8 degrees centigrade by the end of the 21st century. Simulations project that a 4 degree rise in temperature would eliminate nearly all of the world's glaciers."[3]

Well, so what? Here's so what: "Even the modest sea-level rise seen during the twentieth century led to erosion and the loss of 100 square kilometers of wetlands per year in the U.S. Mississippi River Delta."[4] Know where that is? Louisiana. Those wetlands were God's hurricane protection for places like New Orleans. Maybe there would have been different stories about Hurricane Katrina if we were paying attention to melting glaciers, rising ocean temperatures, and wetland preservation.

Back in 1941 we didn't have CNN to cover the news in Peru when a chunk of glacier ice fell into Lake Palcacocha and caused a flood that killed 7,000 people. Another chunk is poised to fall with just a bit more melting. Today 100,000 people would be threatened.

The World Wildlife Fund reports: "A global sea level rise of 1 meter would inundate 80 percent of the Maldives, displace 24 million people in Bangladesh, India and Indonesia, and completely eliminate the Sundarbans, the world's largest mangrove forest and home to the endangered Royal Bengal Tiger and hundreds of other species."[5]

Meanwhile, when I was in Scotland in the summer of 2004, the airwaves were full of concern over Scotland's famous seabirds. Researchers were hoping it was just a bad year. But the trend has continued in 2005. In a September 2005 article the *Scotsman* reported:

> On St. Kilda, which is owned and run by the NTS [National Trust of Scotland], there was a spectacular breeding failure for puffins, with only 26 per cent of burrows producing chicks, compared with a normal figure of 71 per cent. The kittiwake colony on Canna was another notable casualty, with barely five chicks fledged out of 1,000 pairs. Guillemots, razorbills and Arctic tern were also hit, with the most recent survey on Tiree showing only four guillemot chicks at Ceanna'Mhara, from a total of 2,173 birds. In a normal year, there would be about 1,500 chicks in this colony.[6]

Why is breeding down? Birds are hungry. The eels they like to eat are gone. Why? They, too, are hungry. The plankton they like to eat are gone. Why? The water has gotten too warm.

Consider some of these facts from a pamphlet by the Convention on Biological Diversity,[7] now ratified by the overwhelming majority of countries.

- *Based on current trends, an estimated 34,000 plant and 5,200 animal species—including one in eight of the world's bird species—face extinction.* Suppose one of those 34,000 plants holds the cure for cancer?
- *About 30 percent of breeds of the main farm animal species are currently at high risk of extinction.* Do you suppose God might have had some purpose for all those different species of cattle? Do we let them go just because we haven't figured it out yet?
- *About 45 percent of the Earth's original forests are gone, cleared mostly during the past century.* Deforestation is the second largest source of carbon dioxide emissions in developed countries. Carbon dioxide is the biggest culprit in greenhouse gas emissions, which are the problem children mucking up the ozone layer and changing our climate in ways that we don't understand and can't predict.

Sounds pretty ominous, and it is, although when these things are mentioned in many Christian circles, we just drown out the sound with rants about homosexuality and abortion. Those issues should not be neglected, but they will be a moot point if we don't do something about the massive issues surrounding biodiversity. Soon humans, too, will be too hungry to breed. Or they'll be underwater.

There are success stories. The bald eagle is back from the brink of extinction because individuals were unwilling to let our national symbol die out. If we can muster the energy to care, God will aid our efforts and heal our land. Wolf recovery efforts in Yellowstone are also showing incredible results. Ranchers fought it and dire stories were told about potential wolf attacks and other horrible consequences. But the *National Geographic News* had a different report, a scant 8 years after the 1995 reintroduction of 31 wolves. By the end of 2001 there were 220 wolves in 21 packs.[8] Is that good news? Yes. A pack of wolves can bring down a 700 pound elk. That pack of wolves eats only about 20 pounds of it. They go to sleep off their meal and while they doze, in come golden eagles, magpies, coyotes, and other animal scavengers. Those other populations begin to flourish.

Human hunters don't leave that bounty. They leave up to 73,000 pounds of entrails from dressed carcasses over just a six-week period. But the scavengers don't have freezers to store the leftovers for the lean months, so it's either feast or famine. Wolves eat all year round and, therefore, so do the others.

And it's not just other animal species that benefit. Without the threat of wolves, overgrazing is a problem. During the twentieth century there was a noticeable decline in mature aspen, willow, and cottonwood trees. The decline began soon after the extermination of Yellowstone's last wolf pack in 1926. That decline also led to a decline in the beaver population.[9]

Since 1997, the situation has changed. The cottonwood and willow, at least, are on the rebound as elk no longer feel free to hang out by the riverbank and eat them.[10]

These are all issues of covetousness, of greed. We want more and more without any limits placed on our consumption or any concern for the goods which rightly belong to our neighbors. As a nation we've thumbed our noses at the world by refusing to sign the Kyoto Protocol to do our part to curb practices that lead to climate change. A guide to the Kyoto Protocol published by the United Nations Environment Program puts it this way:

Global warming is a particularly ominous example of humanity's insatiable appetite for natural resources. During the last century we have dug up and burned massive stores of coal, oil, and natural gas that took millions of years to accumulate. Our ability to burn up fossil fuels at a rate that is much, much faster than the rate at which they were created has upset the natural balance of the carbon cycle. The threat of climate change arises because one of the only ways the atmosphere—also a natural resource—can respond to the vast quantities of carbon being liberated from beneath the earth's surface is to warm up.

Meanwhile, human expectations are not tapering off. They are increasing. The countries of the industrialized "North" have 20 per cent of the world's people but use about 80 per cent of the world's resources.[11]

We like to call that "growth," "economic development," and "free trade." Scripture calls it "greed," "selfishness," and "pride."

Sure, the Kyoto Protocol isn't perfect. But if we won't sign it because it is flawed, what are we offering in its place? Nothing but more greenhouse gases. We've even managed to invent our own. Sulfur hexafluoride is a man-made gas used as an electrical insulator, heat conductor, and freezing agent. We would be better off with the carbon dioxide. Sulfur hexafluoride has an almost 24,000 times greater potential for increasing global warming.[12]

But we can still do something. International conventions and protocols exist with good recommendations for reversing damage and averting catastrophic harm to many parts of the globe. But those solutions would require us to do with less—to take up our cross and follow rather than charging ahead and trampling all in our path. They would require us rich folks to take some of that personal responsibility we always accuse the poor of not taking and to clean up our own mess. We are a covetous people. It is time to change.

Fair Trade

In the summer of 2004 I spent some sabbatical time in Scotland. I visited the town of Aberfeldy, whose residents boasted that they were the first fair trade town in Scotland. I'd never heard of a fair trade town and had only a vague notion that there was something called fair trade coffee and that it was a good thing to get it.

And yet here I was in a country where there was a whole movement afoot. Edinburgh was working on becoming the first fair trade city, and there were companies that specialized in fair trade goods, from consumables like coffee, tea, and bananas to the durable goods of clothing, jewelry, and furniture.

Fair trade seeks to end covetousness by selling goods produced by fairly paid and justly treated labor. Often this is combined with concern for the sustainability of the environment from which the item came. So coffee growers are not only paid a fair wage for what they grow, they are shown how to grow their crop in the shade so that trees are preserved, and natural predators provide pest control to lessen the use of insecticides. Fair trade journals are printed on recycled paper to help the environment, and fair trade practices help to support the small business owner by providing a fair price for the goods.

When I've raised the idea of a church simply serving fair trade coffee at its functions, the immediate reaction is always a concern that it will cost more. Of course there are always some who see the larger picture, but the bottom line in America is how much an item costs in dollars, not in human lives. Society doesn't have to be structured this way. An anecdote from ancient Gaelic culture tells us this story:

> One of these was a young man of a very ingenious turn of mind. He spent years inventing a machine that would work on a principle somewhat like that of the powerloom which afterwards came . . . he gave a demonstration to his neighbours and asked their opinion about the machine. One of them replied: "Yes, you have invented a wonderful machine. It will make weaving easy. It will save a great deal of labour. But, believe me, in the days to come your name will be execrated for taking away the means of livelihood of so many poor people." Next day, it is said, the young man smashed to pieces the invention . . . [13]

That's what's at the heart of fair trade, and with that story told as part of Gaelic culture, it's no wonder that Scotland is a world leader in the fair trade movement. In Scotland it is a story told with pride. In many quarters in America it would be a story told in scorn, a stupid act that impeded progress. That workers be treated fairly and that the poor be of primary concern are fundamental principles in the Law of Moses, the teaching of the prophets, and the life of Jesus. Are we truly so bent at the altar of Mammon that even Christians are incapable of seeing?

I love the creed of the United Church of Canada. It begins, "We are not alone. We live in God's world." That is God's honest truth, and yet

American Christians often behave as if we were alone and as if the world were ours to use as we see fit, thinking that a sudden Rapture will spare us from the destruction that we have wrought by our thoughtlessness. We do not own the world and all that is in it. God is the owner. The owner will return. I think the owner will want an accounting.

■0■0■

So many of our problems stem from our overweening desires, our covetousness. We want what we want when we want it, and we would prefer to at least delay payment. But the Kingdom of God has a different set of standards. There, the first shall be last, and abundant life comes when we deny ourselves and take up a cross. At least in America, there's not a whole lot of self-denial going on.

The problem isn't desire as much as it is our inability or unwillingness to submit those desires to a higher authority. If we want to covet less, the fruits of the Spirit (Gal 5:22–23) that counteract this are patience and self-control. Maybe there's more patience in the place where you live, but I don't see a lot of it. I don't see a lot of it in my own house, and I'm the only one who lives here. I also completely hate the thought of praying for it, because the more I pray for patience, the more God puts opportunities for patience in my way, which means my desires are thwarted, and I don't like it one little bit. But those painful lessons may, in the end, be what saves me.

11

What Does the Lord Require?

He has told you, O mortal, what is good; and what
does the Lord require of you but to do justice, and to
love kindness, and to walk humbly with your God?
—MICAH 6:8

In serving on the Board of Ordained Ministry in my denomination, I participated in a lot of interviews with candidates seeking ordination. One of the things our interviewing teams always wanted to find out was whether a candidate had a good sense of the difference between acts of justice and acts of mercy.

An act of mercy would be to give a coat to a woman who had none. An act of justice goes a step further by asking, "Why does this woman have no coat?" and then addressing the cultural or systemic issues that might be revealed. Perhaps she has no coat because she is homeless and every time someone gives her a coat, someone else steals it. Perhaps she has no coat because she has Alzheimer's with no one to care for her and is always leaving it somewhere. Perhaps she has no coat because she can't afford one on her minimum-wage salary.

One of the things I have found in ministry is that most churches are much better at acts of mercy than acts of justice. We give food to the food pantries, flood buckets to the hurricane victims, toys and diapers to children in shelters—and well we should. Acts of mercy like that are clearly called for in the Bible.

But one of the things that leads to "mission burnout" in some churches is the sense that people are giving into a black hole. The food we gave got people through today, but every tomorrow they're back, still in need of food, and sometimes we blame the recipients. "We stopped helping Helen. She kept coming back every month for food vouchers. And she went to all the other churches, too." Very few congregations stop to ask why Helen can't get back on her feet—if she was ever on her feet to begin with. We instinctively know that our aid should be just one piece in an overall plan to help a person live a happy and fulfilled life, but we often leave it to someone else to figure out the other parts of the plan. And "someone else" is often no one else.

It's true that government, as the entity that structures our society, has a role to play. But it's up to the citizens of a democratic government to provide guidance for that structure. Those dealing most directly with those in need are best equipped to see the overarching problems that keep people caught in cycles of poverty and want. More than that, acts of justice are as loudly called for in the Bible as are acts of mercy.

If you took the call for acts of justice out of Scripture, there'd be virtually nothing left of the books of the prophets, and if we heeded those prophetic calls, there would be no need for the destruction in the book of Revelation. Jesus calls the Scribes and the Pharisees to return to justice in their dealing with the elderly (Mark 7:11) and overturns the tables of the moneychangers in the Temple (John 2:13–17). If you cut out justice passages you would also lose huge chunks of the Law of Moses, since the laws that God gives to ancient Israel are designed to ensure justice for all levels of society, even to the ox which is not to be muzzled when working to grind meal (Deut 25:4).

If congregations put as much energy into acts of justice as they do into acts of mercy, we could make a true and lasting difference in our world. There's so much creativity sitting in the pews, and those disciples of Jesus Christ work in—and have influence in—all sectors of society. I don't have the answers for how we should solve every social problem, but together as the Body of Christ, with Jesus as our head, I believe we do.

To become a people who both do justice and love mercy, however, we must heed the last point in Micah's trinity. We must walk humbly with God. That was one of the most critical points of Jesus' ministry. Humility. When you pray, go into the closet and close the door. When you give alms, don't brag. Paul so beautifully sums up the "mind of Christ" in Philippians 2:6–8: "Who, though he was in the form of God, did not regard equality with God as something to be exploited, but emptied himself, taking the form of a slave, being born in human likeness. And being found in human form, he humbled himself and became obedient to the point of death—even death on a cross."

It seems to me that in our polarized nation, Christians on both sides have tossed humility out the window. Our side is absolutely right and the other side is absolutely wrong. It's not the issues that polarize us—it's our lack of humility. There can be no dialogue if I can't admit there might be room for growth in my position.

This is where all Christian discussion needs to begin. It is the "mind of Christ," and Paul says it needs to be our mind as well. We can tackle every one of these issues if we can manage enough humility to work together for love of God, neighbor, and self. Working together is, in itself, an act of humility because it acknowledges that we can't do it on our own.

Paul's metaphor of the Body is so important here. "But speaking the truth in love, we must grow up in every way into him who is the head, into Christ, from whom the whole body, joined and knit together by every ligament with which it is equipped, as each part is working properly, promotes the body's growth in building itself up in love" (Eph 4:15–16). That's exactly the point. God has designed us to work together, not to be lone rangers. We're supposed to work together as communities, but also together across communities.

My congregation may have a great ministry to the poor, including a food pantry and a clothes closet, but neither the people nor the funding to do more. That's fine. That may be the particular gift of my part of the Body of Christ. But my congregation, so heavily involved in acts of mercy, should work closely with another church devoted to the justice side of the equation.

Let the justice church spend some time getting to know the people who make use of the services of the mercy church, to discover what systems or laws are preventing them from making headway. Let's say that by working together with the mercy church, the justice church learns that most of the people receiving services are working poor and that the issue is the lack of a living wage. Both churches now have investment in seeing a legal change to the minimum wage.

If the wage were higher, the ministries of the mercy church both could go further and make a larger difference. As a result, those who gave to those ministries would feel better about what they were doing. The justice church also benefits, not only by accomplishing an important goal, but by being able to put a human face on the broad issue they address. Knowing that you helped "people" is important. Knowing that you helped Hal and Kristen and little Kylee is the thing that really makes your heart sing.

Why isn't that sort of cooperation between churches more common? Suppose we took more time as congregations to find our collective place in the Body of Christ? We inventory the spiritual gifts of our members, and we should. But for the same reason that knowing our individual spiritual gifts is a key to successful ministry in local churches, our larger communities can benefit from entire congregations figuring out what God has specifically gifted and called them to do.

It can't be done without humility. To allow that my church is strong in this area but not in that area means that some visitors might join your church instead of mine. In the long run, however, it is freedom—freedom to do what God has called me to do, freedom to see a vision for a particular congregation that can be named, budgeted, and accomplished, freedom to realize that there is no "my church" or "your church," but only the one Church of Jesus Christ to which we all belong. One body, many members.

Right now the Body is pretty much paralyzed. The left leg is trying to go one way, while the right leg tries to saw off the left one so it can go its own way. "The eye cannot say to the hand, 'I have no need of you,' nor again the head to the feet, 'I have no need of you' (1 Cor 12:21). But isn't that what we're saying these days? Republicans say to Democrats, "I have no need of you." Pro-choice says to pro-life, "I have no need of you." Baptist says to Catholic, "I have no need of you." Episcopalian says to Pentecostal, "I have no need of you."

That is neither humble nor correct. If the Body of Christ is to live and move on the earth, the various limbs and organs must find their function and get with the program. The arm can't try to stop the blood flow to the fingers without doing itself great harm. Conservatives can't oust liberals from the Body and expect that the Body will function—and vice versa. We need to do justice. Check. We need to love mercy. Check. And we need to walk humbly with our God. Oops.

We need God. We need each other. It's only together that we can bring God's salvation to the world. Ultimately, that's what this book is about. I've raised enough issues and taken enough personal positions that you probably agreed with some and are ready to tar and feather me for others. I know I've left things out, and I'm sure God will be working on me to change some positions I hold. But the point hasn't been to define God's will for an issue.

The point has been to say that Christians have had tunnel vision when it comes to what constitutes a "moral issue." When Katrina stormed ashore on that late August morning in 2005, the mask was ripped from our national face and we caught a glimpse of what was really underneath. For a moment, at least, the nation saw some of the other moral issues that haven't received much energetic attention.

We saw that nobody thinks to make plans for the poor, the elderly, or the disabled. We saw the contrasting captions on pictures where white people carrying bread were "finding" it in stores while black people carrying bread were "looting." We saw that neglect and development of the wetlands in the Mississippi delta had stolen God's natural protection from a low-lying city. We saw that some people in government get big jobs because of who they know, even if they have no qualifications. We saw that regulations and red tape can cause death. We saw that even if you're hospitalized, lack of insurance will put you on the bottom of the rescue list.

There were, of course, individual acts of heroism and kindness. But, unlike the days that followed 9/11, those acts of kindness weren't the things that impressed us most. Instead we were struck by the collective wake-up call to the other moral issues—the systemic evils of our governmental, corporate, and cultural structures that we had hoped would simply be washed away by the flood.

This is a call to Christians not to forget. This is God's earth and we are all stewards of it and of each other. We can't simply be stewards of one or two issues. We have to open up and face the fact that we are all commandment breakers and that we have both created and participated in systems that often make it impossible for us to keep the commandments God has set before us.

We can change that. We can be in dialogue together, even if we disagree. I'm not talking about Ann Coulter or Michael Moore rants. I'm talking about real conversation where those with differing opinions actually talk calmly and listen to each other, recognizing that we have a faith that unites us beyond all our social positions. If we will put our pride in a closet and quit trying to kick other parts of the Body out of the Kingdom, the Body can begin to function as God intended. Christ is the head of the Body, not us. We can't do it without God, but with God's help, we can begin to address even the most difficult issues with humility, wisdom, and grace, "until all of us come to the unity of the faith and of the knowledge of the Son of God, to maturity, to the measure of the full stature of Christ" (Eph 4:13).

Or not. It's our choice.

Notes

Introduction

1. Everyone thinks it was Florida that defeated Al Gore and put Bush in the White House in the year 2000. It was not. It was the populous and independent-minded New Hampshire Seacoast, where I lived. They cast their votes for Ralph Nader, allowing the state to tilt red by a very small margin in 2000. If the Seacoast votes had gone to Gore, New Hampshire's four electoral votes would have tipped the scale in the other direction. They learned their lesson and did just that in 2004 and the state went blue.

1: No Other Gods

1. Eberhard Arnold, *The Early Christians in Their Own Words*. (Farmington, Pa.: The Plough Publishing House, Fourth Edition, 1997), 15–16.

2. James A. Joseph, "Ethics and Diplomacy: What I Learned from Nelson Mandela" (lecture, Chautauqua Institute, Chautauqua, NY, June 29, 2004).

3. Ibid.

4. Ibid., 5.

5. Ibid., 6.

6. John W. Baur, "The Pledge of Allegiance: A Short History," online adaptation from the author's larger work *The Pledge of Allegiance, A Centennial History 1892–1992* (Annapolis, Md.: Free State Press, Inc., 1992).

7. Religious Tolerance.org, religioustolerance.org/nat_pled1.htm.

2: No Graven Images

1. Stephen Leahy, "Ban Endures on Terminator Seeds," Inter Press Service News Agency, Feb. 11, 2005.

2. Percy Schmeiser's personal website, "Monsanto vs. Schmeiser: The Conflict," www.percyschmeiser.com/conflict.htm.

3. "Monsanto vs. U.S. Farmers: A Report by the Center for Food Safety" (Washington, D.C., 2005): 6.

4. John Vidal, "Canada Backs Terminator Seeds," *The Guardian (UK)*, February 9, 2005.

5. Todd Benson, "Brazil Passes Law Allowing Crops with Modified Genes," *New York Times*, March 4, 2005.

6. Ibid.

7. Margaret R. McLean, "The Future of Food: An Introduction to the Ethical Issues in Genetically Modified Foods" (lecture at a conference entitled "The Future of Food: Legal and Ethical Challenges," Markkula Center for Applied Ethics at Santa Clara University, April 15, 2005).

8. Human Genome Project website, "Genetics and Patenting," http://www.ornl.gov/sci/techresources/Human_Genome/elsi/patents.shtml.

3: Taking God's Name in Vain

1. Madeleine Albright, "The Mighty and the Almighty: United States Foreign Policy and God" (speech, Yale University, March 30, 2004). As quoted in *Context*, June 2005, part A, vol. 37, no. 6.

2. Ibid.

4: Remember the Sabbath

1. Walter J. Harrelson, *Disciple: Becoming Disciples Through Bible Study.*, 2nd ed. (Nashville: Abingdon Press, 1993), video segment for lesson 6.

2. Wayne Muller, *Sabbath: Restoring the Sacred Rhythm of Rest* (New York: Bantam Books, 1999), 111–112.

3. Noam Chomsky, "Jubilee 2000," *ZNet*, May 15, 1998.

4. David Swanson, "Debt Slavery: What the Bankruptcy Bill Could Do to You," April 1, 2005, www.peaceandjustice.org.

5. USDA Forest Service, "Forests on the Edge: Housing Development on America's Private Forests," report fact sheet, May 2005.

6. Ibid.

7. Food Animal Concerns website, "Nest Eggs Meets Its Goals," www.fact.cc/NEMain.htm.

6: Life and Death

1. Death Penalty Information Center, 1101 Vermont Avenue NW, Suite 701, Washington, DC 20005. "Facts About the Death Penalty, fact sheet, October 1, 2005.

7: Be Faithful

1. U.S. Immigration and Customs Enforcement, "Fact Sheet: Internet Child Pornographers," revised July 19, 2005.
2. Ibid.
3. Chicago Coalition for the Homeless, "The Commercial Sexual Exploitation of Homeless Youth," fact sheet, 2003.
4. Ibid.
5. U.S. Department of State, Bureau of Public Affairs, "The Link Between Prostitution and Sex Trafficking," November 24, 2004.
6. U.S. Department of State, International Information Programs, "U.S. Cooperates with Europe to Combat Sex Trafficking. Fact Sheet: U.S. assistance in combating sex trafficking," January 6, 2005, www.usinfo.state.gov.
7. Ibid.

8: Whose Is It, Anyway?

1. Arnold, 14.
2. Ibid, 15.
3. The Trust for Public Land, "No Place to Play: A Comparative Analysis of Park Access in Seven Major Cities" report, November 2004, 6.
4. Ibid, 8.
5. Ibid.
6. Figure from Kissinger Bigatel & Brower Realtors, State College, PA.
7. Peter Fronczek, "Income, Earnings, and Poverty from the 2004 American Community Survey," U.S. Census Bureau, American Community Survey Reports, August 2005, 2.
8. Ibid, 7.
9. Ibid, 9.
10. Joseph, 3.

9: False Witness

1. John Stockwell, *In Search of Enemies* (New York: W.W. Norton & Co., 1978), 13. Book excerpt published on www.thirdworldtraveler.com.

2. Arthur S. Hulnick and Daniel W. Mattausch, "Ethics and Morality in United States Secret Intelligence," *Harvard Journal of Law & Public Policy* 12/2 (Spring 1989), 520–521.

3. H. H. A. Cooper and Lawrence J. Redlinger, *Making Spies: A Talent Spotter's Handbook* (Boulder, Colo.: Paladin, 1986), 108.

4. David L. Perry, "'Repugnant Philosophy': Ethics, Espionage, and Covert Action," *Journal of Conflict Studies* (Spring 1995), 6. As reprinted on http://home .earthlink.net/~daividlperry/covert.htm.

5. Ibid, 8–9.

6. Stockwell, 3.

7. Ibid, 13–14.

8. Arnold, 103–104.

9. Ibid, 103.

10. HALT Fact Sheet. Jeffrey M. Jones, "Nurses Remain Atop Honesty and Ethics List," Gallup News Service (December 5, 2005).

11. Columbia Law School, "Americans Find Lawyers Necessary, But Overpaid and Dishonest," *Lawyers and the Legal Profession*, press release (April 2002).

12. Thanks to the Family Violence Prevention Fund for the collection of much of this data.

13. Bureau of Justice Statistics Crime Data Brief, "Intimate Partner Violence, 1993–2001," February 2003.

14. Patricia Tjaden and Nancy Thoennes, "Prevalence, Incidence, and Consequences of Violence Against Women: Findings from the National Violence Against Women Survey," report, National Institute of Justice and Centers for Disease Control and Prevention, November 1998.

15. Bureau of Justice Statistics Crime Data Brief, "Intimate Partner Violence, 1993–2001," February 2003.

16. I. Horon and D. Cheng, "Enhanced Surveillance for Pregnancy-Associated Mortality—Maryland, 1993–1998," *The Journal of the American Medical Association* 285, no. 11 (March 21, 2001).

17. CDC National Center for Injury Prevention and Control, "Child Maltreatment: Fact Sheet," September 7, 2005. 1

18. Ibid.

19. Karen Scott Collins, Cathy Schoen, Susan Joseph, et al., *Health Concerns Across a Woman's Lifespan: 1998 Survey of Women's Health*, report, The Commonwealth Fund, May 1999.

20. Children Now/Kaiser Permanente poll, December 1995.

10: Thou Shalt Not Covet

1. The Convention on Biological Diversity, "Sustaining Life on Earth: The Role of Science, Technology, and Technical Expertise," brochure from the Secretariat of the Convention on Biological Diversity (n.d.).

2. Ibid.

3. Stacey Combes, Michael L. Prentice, Lara Hansen, and Lynn Rosentrater, "Climate Change Impacts: The Global Glacier Decline," report, World Wildlife Fund, April 25, 2006.

4. Ibid., 5.

5. Ibid., 5 n. 4.

6. John Ross, "Concern at falling seabird numbers," *Scotsman*, September 20, 2005.

7. Secretariat of the Convention on Biological Diversity, "Sustaining life on Earth: How the Convention on Biological Diversity promotes nature and human well-being," April 2000.

8. John Pickrell, "Wolves' Leftovers Are Yellowstone's Gain, Study Says," *National Geographic News*, December 4, 2003.

9. Ibid, 2.

10. Ibid.

11. United Nations Environment Programme and Climate Change Secretariat, "Understanding Climate Change: A Beginner's Guide to the UN Framework Convention and Its Kyoto Protocol," booklet, September 1999, 16; revised July 2002.

12. Ibid, 22.

13. Michael Newton, *A Handbook of the Scottish Gaelic World* (Portland, Ore.: Four Courts Press, 2000), 260.

Further Reading

No Other Gods

Albright, Madeleine. *The Mighty and the Almighty: Reflections on America, God, and World Affairs.* New York: HarperCollins, 2006.

Robertson, Anne. *Blowing the Lid Off the God-Box: Opening Up to a Limitless Faith.* Harrisburg, PA: Morehouse Publishing, 2005.

Walzer, Michael. *Politics and Passion: Toward a More Egalitarian Liberalism.* New Haven, CT: Yale University Press, 2005.

Wink, Walter. *Engaging the Powers: Discernment and Resistance in a World of Domination.* Minneapolis: Fortress, 1992.

The Bottom Line

Arena, Christine. *Cause for Success: 10 Companies That Put Profit Second and Came in First.* Novato, CA: New World Library, 2004.

Frank, Thomas. *One Market Under God: Extreme Capitalism, Market Populism, and the End of Economic Democracy.* New York: Anchor, 2001.

Gunther, Marc. *Faith and Fortune: The Quiet Revolution to Reform American Business.* New York: Crown Business, 2004.

Litvin, Daniel. *Empires of Profit: Commerce, Conquest, and Corporate Responsibility.* London: Texere, 2003.

The National Interest

Carter, Jimmy. *Our Endangered Values: America's Moral Crisis.* New York: Simon & Schuster, 2005.

Hehir, Bryan J., ed. *Liberty and Power: A Dialogue on Religion and U.S. Foreign Policy in an Unjust World.* Washington, DC: Brookings Institution, 2004.

Kissinger, Henry. *Diplomacy*. Reprint edition. New York: Simon & Schuster, 1995.

Lang, Anthony F. Jr., ed. *Just Intervention*. Washington, DC: Georgetown University Press, 2003.

Lebow, Richard Ned. *The Tragic Vision of Politics: Ethics, Interests and Orders*. New York: Cambridge University Press, 2003.

Freedom

Dworkin, Ronald. *Freedom's Law: The Moral Reading of the American Constitution*. Cambridge, MA: Harvard University Press, 1997.

Zakaria, Fareed. *The Future of Freedom: Illiberal Democracy at Home and Abroad*. New York: W. W. Norton, 2004.

Gun Control

Jacobs, James B. *Can Gun Control Work?* New York: Oxford University Press, 2002.

Nisbet, Lee. *The Gun Control Debate: You Decide*. Second edition. Amherst, NY: Prometheus, 2001.

Hate Speech

Gould, Jon B. *Speak No Evil: The Triumph of Hate Speech Regulation*. Chicago: University of Chicago Press, 2005.

Stone, Geoffrey R. *Perilous Times: Free Speech in Wartime from the Sedition Act of 1798 to the War on Terrorism*. New York: W. W. Norton, 2004.

Pledge of Allegiance

Baer, John. *The Pledge of Allegiance: A Centennial History 1892–1992*. Annapolis, MD: Free State, 1992.

No Graven Images

Smith, Huston. *The Soul of Christianity: Restoring the Great Tradition*. San Francisco: HarperSanFrancisco, 2005.

The Ten Commandments

Derschowitz, Alan M. *The Genesis of Jusitce: Ten Stories of Biblical Injustice that Led to the Ten Commandments and Modern Law*. New York: Warner, 2001.

Hauerwas, Stanley and William Willimon. *The Truth About God: The Ten Commandments in Christian Life*. Nashville: Abingdon, 1999.

Hester, Joseph P. *The Ten Commandments: A Handbook of Religious, Legal, and Social Issues*. Jefferson, NC: McFarland, 2003.

Creationism and Evolution

Larson, Edward J. *Summer for the Gods: The Scopes Trial and America's Continuing Debate Over Science and Religion*. Reprint edition. Cambridge, MA: Harvard University Press, 1998.

Scott, Eugenie. *Evolution vs. Creationism: An Introduction*. Berkeley: University of California Press, 2005.

Witham, Larry. *The Measure of God: Our Century-Long Struggle to Reconcile Science & Religion*. San Francisco: HarperSanFrancisco, 2005.

Republican or Democrat?

Campolo, Tony. *Speaking My Mind: The Radical Evangelical Prophet Tackles the Tough Issues Christians Are Afraid to Face*. Nashville: W. Publishing Group, 2004.

Wallis, Jim. *God's Politics: Why the Right Gets It Wrong and the Left Doesn't Get It*. San Francisco: HarperSanFrancisco, 2005.

Genetic Engineering

Shannon, Thomas A. *Made in Whose Image: Genetic Engineering and Christian Ethics*. Detroit: Humanity, 1999.

Watson, James D., and Andrew Berry. *DNA: The Secret of Life*. New York: Knopf, 2003.

Taking God's Name in Vain

Evangelism

Hunter, George G. III. *The Celtic Way of Evangelism: How Christianity Can Reach the West . . . Again*. Nashville: Abingdon, 2000.

Morgenthaler, Sally. *Worship Evangelism: Inviting Unbelievers into the Presence of God*. Grand Rapids, MI: Zondervan, 1999.

Baptism

Stookey, Laurence Hull. *Baptism: Christ's Act in the Church*. Nashville: Abingdon, 1982.

Christian Nation

Church, Forrest. *The Separation of Church and State: Writings on a Fundamental Freedom by America's Founders.* Boston: Beacon, 2004.

Gonzalez, Justo L. *Church History: An Essential Guide.* Nashville: Abingdon, 1996.

Hauerwas, Stanley. *After Christendom: How the Church Is to Behave if Freedom, Justice, and a Christian Nation Are Bad Ideas.* Nashville: Abingdon, 1991.

Remember the Sabbath

Heschel, Abraham Joshua. *The Sabbath.* New York: Farrar, Straus and Giroux, 1975.

Muller, Wayne. *Sabbath: Restoring the Sacred Rhythm of Rest.* New York: Bantam, 1999

Capitalism

Prahalad, C. K. *The Fortune at the Bottom of the Pyramid: Eradicating Poverty through Profits.* Upper Sadie River, NJ: Wharton School, 2004.

Hart, Stuart L. *Capitalism at the Crossroads: The Unlimited Business Opportunities in Solving the World's Most Difficult Problems.* Upper Sadie River: Wharton School, 2005.

Hauerwas, Stanley. *A Better Hope: Resources for a Church Confronting Capitalism, Democracy, and Post-Modernity.* Reprint edition. Gramd Rapids: Brazos, 2000.

The Land

Kimbrell, Andrew. *Fatal Harvest: The Tragedy of Industrial Agriculture.* Fort Cronkhite, CA: Foundation for Deep Ecology, 2002

Wirzba, Norman, and Barbara Kingsolver. *The Essential Agrarian Reader: The Future of Culture, Community, and the Land.* Emeryville, CA: Shoemaker and Hoard, 2004.

Humane Farming

Cook, Christopher D. *Diet for a Dead Planet: How the Food Industry Is Killing Us.* New York: New Press, 2004.

Schlosser, Eric. *Fast Food Nation: The Dark Side of the All-American Meal.* London: Harper Perennial, 2005.

Honor Thy Father and Mother

Health Care

Bartlett, Donald L., and James B. Steele. *Critical Condition: How Health Care in America Became Big Business—and Bad Medicine.* New York: Doubleday, 2004.

Lamm, Richard D. *The Brave New World of Health Care.* Golden, CO: Fulcrum, 2003.

Ageism

Butler, Robert N. *Why Survive? Being Old in America.* Baltimore: Johns Hopkins University Press, 2003.

Rowe, John W., and Robert L. Kahn. *Successful Aging.* New York: Dell, 1999.

Our Faith Parents

Harrelson, Walter, and Randall M. Falk. *Jews and Christians: A Troubled Family.* Nashville: Abingdon, 1990.

Wilson, Marvin R. *Our Father Abraham: Jewish Roots of the Christian Faith.* Grand Rapids, MI: Eerdmans, 1989.

Williams, Daniel H. *Retrieving the Tradition and Renewing Evangelicalism: A Primer for Suspicious Protestants.* Grand Rapids, MI: Eerdmans, 1999.

Life and Death

Niebuhr, Reinhold. *Love and Justice: Selections from the Shorter Writings of Reinhold Niebuhr.* Louisville, KY: Westminster John Knox, 1992.

Stem Cell Research

Ruse, Michael, and Christopher A. Pynes, eds. *The Stem Cell Controversy: Debating the Issues.* Amherst, NY: Prometheus, 2003.

Waters, Brent, and Ronald Cole Turner, eds. *God and the Embryo: Religious Voices on Stem Cells and Cloning.* Washington, DC: Georgetown University Press, 2003.

Abortion

Alcorn, Randy. *Pro-Life Answers to Pro-Choice Arguments.* Expanded edition. Sisters, OR: Multnomah, 2000.

Baird, Robert M., and Stuart E. Rosenbaum, eds. *The Ethics of Abortion: Pro-Life Vs. Pro-Choice*. Third edition. Amherst, NY: Prometheus, 2001.

Judges, Donald. *Hard Choices, Lost Voices: How the Abortion Conflict Has Divided America, Distorted Constitutional Rights, and Damaged the Courts*. Chicago: Ivan R. Dee, Publisher, 1993.

Solinger, Rickie, ed. *Abortion Wars: A Half Century of Struggle, 1950–2000*. Berkeley: University of California Press, 1998.

Euthanasia

Dowbiggin, Ian Robert. *A Merciful End: The Euthanasia Movement in Modern America*. New York: Oxford University Press, 2002.

Moreno, Jonathan. *Arguing Euthanasia: The Controversy Over Mercy-Killing, Assisted Suicide and the "Right to Die."* New York: Touchstone, 1995.

War

Nardin, Terry, ed. *The Ethics of War and Peace*. Reprint Edition. Princeton, NJ: Princeton University Press, 1998.

Temes, Peter. *The Just War: An American Reflection on the Morality of War in Our Time*. Chicago: Ivan R. Dee, Publisher, 2003.

Walzer, Michael. *Arguing About War*. New Haven, CT: Yale University Press, 2004.

Yoder, John Howard. *The Politics of Jesus*. Second edition. Grand Rapids, MI: Eerdman's, 1994.

Capital Punishment

Bedau, Hugo Adam, and Paul G. Cassell, eds. *Debating the Death Penalty: Should America Have Capital Punishment? The Experts on Both Sides Make Their Best Case*. New York: Oxford University Press, 2003.

Owens, Erik C., John D. Carlson, and Eric P. Elshtain, eds. *Religion and the Death Penalty: A Call for Reckoning*. Grand Rapids, MI: Eerdmans, 2004.

Hunting and Vegetarianism

Linzey, Andrew. *Animal Gospel*. Louisville, KY: Westminster John Knox, 1998.

Rice, Pamela. *101 Reasons Why I'm a Vegetarian*. New York: Lantern, 2004.

Scully, Matthrew. *Dominion: The Power of Man, the Suffering of Animals, and the Call to Mercy*. New York: St. Martin's Griffin, 2003.

Be Faithful

Marriage and Relationships

Coontz, Stephanie. *Marriage, A History: From Obedience to Intimacy, or How Love Conquered Marriage*. New York: Viking Adult, 2005.

Gaillardetz, Richard R. *A Daring Promise: A Spirituality of Christian Marriage*. New York: Crossroad General Interest, 2002.

Hendrix, Harville. *Getting the Love You Want: A Guide for Couples*. Reprint edition. New York: Owl, 2001.

Richo, David. *How to Be an Adult in Relationships: The Five Keys to Mindful Loving*. Boston: Shambhala, 2002.

Marriage and Sexuality

Balswick, Judith K., and Jack O. Balswick. *Authentic Human Sexuality: An Integrated Christian Approach*. Downer's Grove, IL: InterVarsity, 2000.

Parrinder, Geoffrey. *Sexual Morality in the World's Religions*. Reprint edition. Oxford, England: OneWorld, 1995.

Smedes, Lewis. *Sex for Christians: The Limits and Liberties of Sexual Living*. Revised edition. Grand Rapids, MI: Eerdman's, 1994.

Divorce

Callison, Walter. *Divorce: A Gift of God's Love*. Overland Park, KS: Leathers, 2002.

Fisher, Bruce, and Robert E. Alberti. *Rebuilding: When Your Relationship Ends*. Third edition. New York: Impact, 1999.

Kniskern, Joseph Warren. *When the Vow Breaks: A Survival and Recovery Guide for Christians Facing Divorce*. Nashville: Broadman and Holman, 1993.

Homosexuality

Balch, David L., ed. *Homosexuality, Science, and the "Plain Sense" of Scripture*. Grand Rapids, MI: Eerdmans, 2000.

Boswell, John. *Christianity, Social Tolerance, and Homosexuality: Gay People in Western Europe from the Beginning of the Christian Era to the Fourteenth Century*. Chicago: University of Chicago Press, 2005.

Helminiak, Daniel A. *What the Bible Really Says about Homosexuality*. San Francisco: Alamo Square, 2000.

Gay Marriage

Moats, David. *Civil Wars: A Battle for Gay Marriage*. Orlando, FL: Harcourt, 2004.

Myers, David G., and Letha Dawson Scanzoni. *What God Has Joined Together?: A Christian Case for Gay Marriage*. San Francisco: HarperSanFrancisco, 2005.

Gender Switching—The Transgendered and Transvestite

Fausto-Sterling, Anne. *Sexing the Body: Gender Politics and the Construction of Sexuality*. New York: Basic, 2000.

Myerowitz, Joanne. *How Sex Changed: A History of Transsexuality in the United States*. Cambridge, MA: Harvard University Press, 2004.

Pornography

Paul, Pamela. *Pornified: How Pornography Is Transforming Our Lives, Our Relationships, and Our Families*. Singapore: Times, 2005

Strossen, Nadine. *Defending Pornography: Free Speech, Sex, and the Fight for Women's Rights*. New York: New York University Press, 2000.

Prostitution and Sex Trafficking

Farr, Kathryn. *Sex Trafficking: The Global Market in Women and Children*. New York: Worth, 2004.

Kempadoo, Kamala, Jyoti Sanghera, and Bandana Pattanik, eds. *Trafficking and Prostitution Reconsidered: New Perspectives on Migration, Sex Work, and Human Rights*. Boulder, CO: Paradigm, 2005.

Thou Shalt Not Steal

Private Property

Arnold, Eberhard, ed. *The Early Christians in Their Own Words*. Farmington, PA: The Plough Publishing House, 1997.

Bethell, Tom. *The Noblest Triumph: Property and Prosperity through the Ages*. New York: Palgrave Macmillan, 1999.

Freyfogle, Eric T. *The Land We Share: Private Property and the Public Good*. Washington, DC: Shearwater, 2003.

Pipes, Richard. *Property and Freedom*. New York: Vintage, 2000.

Public Space

Carmona, Matthew, Steven Tiesdell, and Tim Heath. *Public Places—Urban Spaces*. Burlington, MA: Architectural Press, 2003.

Putnam, Robert D. *Bowling Alone: The Collapse and Revival of American Community*. New York: Simon & Schuster, 2001.

Affordable Housing

Grogan, Paul S., and Tony Proscio. *Comeback Cities: A Blueprint for Urban Neighborhood Revival*. Boulder, CO: Westview, 2001.

Hecht, Bennett L. *Developing Affordable Housing: A Practical Guide for Nonprofit Organizations*. Second edition. Indianapolis: Wiley, 1999.

Urban Land Institute, National Building Museum. *Affordable Housing: Designing an American Asset*. Washington, DC: Urban Land Institute, 2005.

Tithing and Faith-Based Initiatives

Dionne, E. J., and John J. Diullio Jr., eds. *What's God Got to Do with the American Experiment?: Essays on Religion and Politics*. Washington, DC: Brookings Institution, 2000.

Webb, Michael L., and Mitchell T. Webb. *Beyond Tithes & Offerings*. Tacoma, WA: On Time, 1998.

Racism

Shearer, Tobin Miller, and Jody Miller Shearer. *Enter the River: Healing Steps from White Privilege toward Racial Reconciliation*. Scottdale, Pennsylvania: Herald, 1994

Takaki, Ronald. *A Different Mirror: A History of Multicultural America*. Back Bay, 1994.

Sexism

Gilligan, Carol. *In a Different Voice: Psychological Theory and Women's Development*. Harvard University Press, 1993

Johnson, Allan G. *The Gender Knot: Unraveling Our Patriarchal Legacy*. Philadelphia: Temple University Press, 1997.

False Witness

Bok, Sissela. *Lying: Moral Choice in Public and Private Life*. New York: Pantheon, 1978; Random House, 1979.

Espionage

Kessler, Ronald. *Inside the CIA*. New York: Pocket, 1994.

Stockwell, John. *In Search of Enemies: A CIA Story*. Bridgewater, NJ: Replica, 1997.

The Legal System

Baker, Thomas E., and Timothy W. Floyd, eds. *Can a Good Christian Be a Good Lawyer?: Homilies, Witnesses, and Reflections*. South Bend, IN: University of Notre Dame Press, 1998.

Harr, Jonathan. *A Civil Action*. Reprint edition. New York: Vintage, 1996.

Rosenbaum, Thane. *The Myth of Moral Justice: Why Our Legal System Fails to Do What's Right*. New York: Perennial, 2005.

Zitrin, Richard A., and Carol M. Langford. *The Moral Compass of the American Lawyer: Truth, Justice, Power, and Greed*. New York: Ballantine, 2000.

Domestic Abuse

Cook, Philip W. *Abused Men*. Westport, CT: Praeger Trade, 1997.

Costin, Lela B., Howard Jacob Karger, and David Stoesz. *The Politics of Child Abuse in America*. Reprint edition. New York: Oxford University Press, 1996.

Stewart, Donald. *Refuge: A Pathway Out of Domestic Violence & Abuse*. Birmingham, AL: New Hope, 2004.

Illegal Immigration

Annerino, John. *Dead in Their Tracks: Crossing America's Desert Borderlands*. New York: Four Walls Eight Windows, 2003.

Conover, Ted. *Coyotes: A Journey Through the Secret World of America's Illegal Aliens*. New York: Vintage, 1987.

Krauss, Erich. *On the Line: Inside the U.S. Border Patrol*. Sacramento: Citadel, 2004.

Sassen, Saskia. *Guests and Aliens*. New York: New Press, 2000.

Thou Shalt Not Covet

Batstone, David. *Saving the Corporate Soul—And (Who Knows?) Maybe Your Own: Eight Principles for Creating and Preserving Wealth and Well-Being for You and Your Company Without Selling Out*. San Francisco: Jossey-Bass, 2003.

Kaza, Stephanie, ed. *Hooked: Buddhist Writings on Greed, Desire, and the Urge to Consume*. Boston: Shambhala, 2005.

Leach, William R. *Land of Desire: Merchants, Power, and the Rise of a New American Culture*. New York: Vintage, 1994.

The Earth's Resources

Diamond, Jared. *Collapse: How Societies Choose to Fail or Succeed*. New York: Viking Adult, 2004.

Meadows, Donella H., Jorgen Randers, and Dennis L. Meadows, eds. *Limits to Growth: The 30-Year Update*. White River Jct., VT: Chelsea Green, 2004.

Biodiversity

American Museum of Natural History and Michael J. Novacek. *The Biodiversity Crisis: Losing What Counts*. New York: New Press, 2001.

Gore, Al. *An Inconvenient Truth: The Planetary Emergency of Global Warming and What We Can Do about It*. Emmaus, PA: Rodale, 2006.

Reaka-Kudla, Marjorie L., Don E. Wilson, and Edward O. Wilson, eds. *Bioiversity II: Understanding and Protecting Our Biological Resources*. Washington, DC: National Academies, 1997.

Wilson, Edward O., ed. *Biodiversity*. Washington, DC: National Academies, 1988.

Fair Trade

Hollender, Jeffrey and Stephen Fenichell. *What Matters Most: How a Small Group of Pioneers Is Teaching Social Responsibility to Big Business, and Why Big Business Is Listening*. New York: Basic, 2003.

Nicholls, Alex, and Charlotte Opal. *Fair Trade: Market-Driven Ethical Consumption*. Thousand Oaks, CA: SAGE, 2005.